# simply
# PRAYING

## 52 weeks with God

Patsy Lewis

BEACON HILL PRESS
OF KANSAS CITY

Cover Design: Darlene Filley
Interior Design: Sharon Page

All Scripture quotations not otherwise designated are from the *Holy Bible, New International Version* (NIV*). Copyright © 1973, 1978, 1984 by International Bible Society. Used by permission of Zondervan Publishing House. All rights reserved.

Permission to quote from the following additional copyrighted versions of the Bible is acknowledged with appreciaton:

*The Message* (TM). Copyright © 1993, 1994, 1995, 1996, 2000, 2001, 2002. Used by permission of NavPress Publishing Group.

*The Holy Bible, New Living Translation* (NLT). Copyright © 1996. Used by permission of Tyndale House Publishers, Inc., Wheaton, IL 60189. All rights reserved.

The *New American Standard Bible®* (NASB®). Copyright © The Lockman Foundation 1960, 1962, 1963, 1968, 1971, 1972, 1973, 1975, 1977, 1995.

*The Living Bible* (TLB), © 1971. Used by permission of Tyndale House Publishers, Inc., Wheaton, IL 60189. All rights reserved.

Scripture quotations marked KJV are from the King James Version.

Library of Congress Cataloging-in-Publicaton Data

Lewis, Patsy, 1942-
  Simply praying : 52 weeks with God / Patsy Lewis.
    p. cm.
  Includes bibliographical references.
  ISBN-13: 978-0-8341-2271-0 (pbk.)
  ISBN-10: 0-8341-2271-5 (pbk.)
  1. Prayer—Christianity. I. Title.

  BV215.L49 2006
  248.3'2—dc22

                                                     2006021154

10 9 8 7 6 5 4 3

# DEDICATION

This book is dedicated to
Marissa Lanea Lewis,
my firstborn grandchild,
who at four years of age prayed a prayer
that inspired this book and changed my life.

# ACKNOWLEDGEMENTS

Special thanks to:

- Joyce Williams for encouraging me to write
- Hardy Weathers for believing in me
- Bonnie Perry, Judi Perry, and Barry Russell at Beacon Hill Press for guiding this project to completion
- Darlene Filley for cover design and Sharon Page for interior design
- Stan and Linda Toler for their friendship and advice
- Marissa Lanea Lewis, Kiersten Michelle Lewis, Makaila Rhea Lewis, Calvin Reid Brantley, and Caleb Clayton Brantley, my grandchildren, for providing many stories for this book
- Kevin Lane Lewis and Lanissa Carol Lewis Brantley, my children, for enriching my life
- Michelle Rhea McGuire Lewis, my wonderful daughter-in-law, and Richard Clayton Brantley II, my dear son-in-law, for loving me and my children
- Curtis Lewis Jr., my husband, for his unconditional love and support of my endeavors
- Michele Smith, my prayer partner for many years, for praying for me daily
- A host of friends who have prayed faithfully for me and my family

# CONTENTS

# FOREWORD

I've known Patsy Lewis for more than 25 years. She has been a wonderful friend to the Toler family. We have felt her prayers and appreciated her encouragement. Patsy is a leader whose walk matches her talk. She truly practices what she writes.

This book, *Simply Praying*, is a reflection of her life and ministry. Patsy has consistently demonstrated a devoted prayer life, and this book is a manual for practical praying.

As you read the book, you will discover the formula for using the scriptures in prayer. Also, her stories of her grandchildren will cause you to smile and to pray with childlike faith.

Her insights on practicing the presence of God, singing to the Lord, writing out prayers, and listening with anticipation seem to echo the words of the disciples when they said, "Lord, teach us to pray."

—Stan Toler, Pastor & Author, Oklahoma City, Oklahoma

# PREFACE

As a child, I thought personal prayer was for mealtime and bedtime. I said a recited blessing before I ate and knelt by my bed to pray before I crawled under the covers each night. Those nightly prayers usually consisted of thanking God for my family and asking Him to bless them. That pattern continued for many years.

A few weeks ago, a mother whose children are grown confessed to me that the only time she prays is just before falling asleep for the night. She added that she sometimes silently asks God to help her through the day before getting out of bed in the morning. She is not alone. A large number of Christians spend little time with the Lord.

Many persons think of personal prayer as kneeling before a bed or chair with their lists of requests. But prayer is much more than that. It is a way of life, an exciting adventure!

The first recording of humankind calling on the name of the Lord is found in Gen. 4:26: "At that time men began to call on the name of the LORD." The Bible is filled with examples of people who modeled prayer:

- Moses sang and prayed a prayer of thanksgiving after leading the children of Israel across the Red Sea on dry land. (Exod. 15)
- Hannah prayed for a child. (2 Sam. 1)
- Solomon prayed a prayer of dedication for the temple. (1 Kings 8)
- Elijah prayed for rain. (1 Kings 18)

- Many of the Psalms are poems and songs that include prayers for help and prayers of praise.
- Both Mary and Zechariah sang their prayers of praise in Luke 1.
- Simeon took Jesus in his arms in the temple and prayed a prayer of praise and thanksgiving. (Luke 2:28-32)

A host of other prayers are found in the Old Testament and New Testament, but Jesus is our greatest example of one who prayed and taught about prayer.

- He fasted and prayed in the wilderness. (Matt. 4, Mark 1, and Luke 4)
- He prayed alone following John the Baptist's death and after feeding the five thousand. (Matt. 14:23)
- He took Peter, James, and John on a mountain to pray. (Luke 9:28)
- He prayed in the Garden of Gethsemane. (Matt. 26:36-42, Mark 14:32-42, Luke 22:39-46)
- He prayed on the cross. (Matt. 27:46, Mark 15:34, Luke 23:34 and 46)

There are many other verses that show us Jesus praying as well as teaching on prayer including Matt. 6:1-18 and Luke 11:1-13.

- He taught His followers to be direct in their requests and not bargain with God in Matt. 7:7-12.
- He acknowledged the power of united prayer in Matt. 18:18-20.
- He said the temple should be a house of prayer in Matt. 21:13.
- The longest recorded prayer of Jesus is His prayer for His disciples and future followers in John 17.

These references to Jesus and prayer in no way exhaust the examples in Scripture. It is clear that Jesus encouraged prayer and considered praying important.

I have led prayer groups for 35 years, conducted prayer seminars, organized prayer retreats, spoken on prayer, written about prayer, directed individuals in prayer walks, and encouraged others to be involved in prayer. It is a privilege to speak to and hear from the Creator of the Universe! Amazing things have happened as I have watched God transform me and others.

My purpose in writing this book is to lead you on a life-changing prayer adventure by suggesting a different prayer focus for each week of the year. The most effective way to use this tool is to read one chapter each week and apply the prayerful suggestions as you explore the scripture for that week. It is not necessary to start on January 1 or even to start on a Monday. Instead, I suggest you start immediately. How about right now? Why don't you get started today?

# INTRODUCTION

When our granddaughter Marissa was four years old, she prayed from the depths of her little heart one evening just before bed. Her words touched me deeply as she prayed, oblivious that anyone but Jesus was listening: "Dear Jesus, I love you. I love you so much that I am just going to run into your arms when I see you!" There was no doubt in her mind that His arms would be outstretched to welcome her.

"Because of Christ and our faith in Him, we can now come fearlessly into God's presence, assured of His glad welcome" (Eph. 3:12, NLT).

Do you get the picture? Jesus is waiting with outstretched arms to welcome you when you come to Him in prayer.

- Come in your shyness; He will not embarrass you.
- Come with your guilt and shame; He will not turn you away.
- Come in your weariness; He will give you rest.
- Come in your despair; He will extend hope.
- Come in your excitement; He will celebrate with you.

Just come.

Here is Christ's spoken invitation to you: "Are you tired? Worn out? Burned out on religion? Come to me. Get away with me, and you'll recover your life. I'll show you how to take a real rest. Walk with me and work with me—watch how I do it. Learn the unforced rhythms of grace. I won't lay anything heavy or ill-fitting on you. Keep company with me and you'll learn to live freely and lightly" (Matt. 11:28-30, TM).

Pause now and reflect on the lyrics of "He Is Here." Remember, the place where you are sitting or standing is holy. Listen for His voice. Feel His touch.

He is here, hallelujah!
He is here, amen!
He is here, holy, holy,
I will bless His name again.
He is here; listen closely.
Hear Him calling out your name.
He is here; you can touch Him.
You will never be the same.*

*Kirk Talley, "He Is Here," © Copyright 1990. Kirk Talley Music/BMI (admin. by ICG). All rights reserved. Used by permission.

# OPEN YOUR HEART

Children teach us powerful truths about prayer! When our son Kevin was nearly four years old, he asked me one night at bedtime prayers to tell Jesus not to come into his heart because he was afraid it might hurt. This became a nightly request as he locked his arms tightly over his heart. I assured Kevin that Jesus would not come until he invited Him, and amazingly, it would not hurt at all. Then I prayed, "Jesus, you understand that Kevin is afraid to have you come into his heart. It seems to him it would hurt. I've assured him you will not come until he is ready, and it really won't hurt, but it helps us to talk to you about it." Night after night, we continued this ritual until one bedtime Kevin said, "I'm ready to ask Jesus into my heart tonight." We prayed a totally different prayer that night.

When Kevin was five, he came home from church one Sunday and reported that some of his friends had asked Jesus into their hearts during children's church that morning. I thought perhaps he was trying to tell me that he, too, had prayed. When I asked him if he was one of those who had asked Jesus into his heart, he emphatically replied, "No, remember, I did that one night when we lived in Champaign!" I assured him that I did remember that night very well, but sometimes people pray again to reassure themselves that

Jesus is still there. Little Kevin turned and put his head down on the kitchen counter where I was preparing lunch, and I asked him if something was wrong. He shook his head no, but he kept his head down resting on his arms. Before long he snapped his head up and quipped cheerfully, "I was just checking to see if He's still there, and He is!"

My son demonstrated several truths about prayer that day:

- We can tell God our fears, doubts, worries, concerns, anything.

- When we listen, we can hear Him.

- Simple prayers are heard and answered.

Perhaps you fear asking Christ Jesus into your heart. I assure you that He will come when you invite Him, and it will not hurt. He brings only peace, freedom, and forgiveness of your sins. If you have never asked Jesus to forgive your sins and come into your heart, that is your first step toward an intimate relationship with Him. Revelation 3:20 says, "Here I am! I stand at the door and knock. If anyone hears my voice and opens the door, I will come in and eat with him, and he with me."

If you have asked Christ into your heart, spend this week reflecting on the first time you sensed God calling you to come to Him. Allow yourself to remember the time when you opened your heart and life to Him. Give thanks for the lessons He has taught you along the journey, for answered prayer, and for the times He has spoken to your heart through scripture, sermons, songs, books, and in your quiet moments with Him.

Read Rev. 3:20 again. The scripture surrounding that verse helps us realize that the passage was written to followers of Christ at the Laodicean Church. Envision Christ knocking at your heart's door to invite you to spend time with Him. He truly is waiting to fellowship with you and impart truth to you. It is important to record the lessons He teaches you on this great adventure with Him.

## Increase Your Spiritual Awareness

Today or tomorrow, purchase a spiral notebook or bound journal. Beautiful journals can be purchased at any bookstore and most discount stores. Begin writing the story of your journey with God.

- Start with your first recollection of His grace extended to you.
- Write about the events surrounding your invitation to Him to come into your life.
- Add details of the highlights of your walk with Christ.
- Include some of the spiritual lessons you have learned along the way.
- Conclude with a paragraph of how you picture your relationship with Christ at the present time.
- Read your story through again, and then share it with someone else.

## Scripture for This Week

(PS. 139)

Read this chapter, or at least a few verses, each day.

Write verses 23-24 on a card to carry with you, and try to memorize them.

## Praying Scripture

(REV. 3:20 AND PS. 139:23-24)

*Dear God,*

*Thank you for inviting me to open my heart for your coming. It humbles me to think that you desire to fellowship with me, that your spirit surrounds me and is within me. I give you permission to examine my heart, even my thoughts. Since you know everything there is to know about me, which is both a frightening and awesome revelation, I desire to have you reveal truth to me. Tell me if there is any wickedness in me that needs your cleansing; I am listening. Lead me on the path to eternal life. Thank you for extending your hand of blessing to me. Amen.*

### Prayer Song from Psalm 139:1-7

O Lord, you have examined my heart.
You know everything there is to know about me.
You know when I stand or sit.
You know every word I speak.
When far away, you know my every thought.
Your Spirit surrounds me every moment of my life.
You chart the path ahead and tell me where to rest.
Every moment, you know where I am.
You both precede me and follow.
You extend your hand of blessing.
This is too glorious, too wonderful to know.
Your spirit surrounds me every moment of my life.

# SHADOW JESUS

Each year I ask God to give me a theme or focus idea for the coming year. It develops in various ways during the weeks leading up to Christmas and my birthday on Christmas Eve. All of these occasions give me opportunities for reflection over the past year and anticipation of the coming year. Sometimes the theme evolves from a book or scripture I am reading.

Earlier this year, I was reading in Acts 5:12-16 about sick people who were brought to the streets on beds and mats so Peter's shadow could fall on them. I began to pray that people who pass through my shadow will be enriched and changed spiritually. As I prayed about a theme for the year, I immediately knew it would be to "Shadow Jesus." To do this, I would bring myself daily into His presence and allow the shadow of His presence to cover me and walk with me throughout the day. I pictured that as I remained close to Him and in His shadow, my shadow reflected His. I wrote in my journal:

> *May I abide in the shadow of your wings, always staying close to you. May I enrich the lives of all on whom my shadow falls.*

My theme the year before was "Gratitude." My goal was to have a grateful heart at all times, in all situations, under all circumstances.

Themes for other years have been: "Live in Love," "Develop a Hearing Heart," "Wear a Crown of Joy at All Times," "Live Each Day So That Christ Will Be Pleased to Sign His Name to It."

I have been choosing a theme for the year for more than 30 years. My list of themes is long. I encourage you to prayerfully ask God to give you a theme, scripture, or special focus for your year of spiritual adventure.

## Increase Your Spiritual Awareness

Spend a few moments reflecting on the past year, and then give the year and its struggles, victories, defeats, joys, and disappointments to God.

This week ponder the idea of a theme or scripture for the year. Keep your heart open as you read the scripture and pray.

## Scripture for This Week

### (ACTS 5 AND PS. 63)

Read Ps. 63 and give praise.

Read Acts 5 several times this week. There are many lessons to be learned from the early followers of Christ. Ask God to speak to you through this scripture. Choose a story, lesson, or response from Acts 5 each day this week, and think about it. Make a list of the lessons you can apply to your own life.

## Praying Scripture

(ACTS 5:41-42 AND PS. 63:4-7)

*Lord,*

*I am not sure I could have rejoiced as the apostles did after they were flogged and then asked not to speak again in the name of Jesus. It challenges me that they were rejoicing because they had been counted worthy of suffering disgrace for your name. Not only did they rejoice, they courageously continued to proclaim your name daily in the temple courts and from house to house. They could not be stopped. This gives me the courage to teach and proclaim the good news that Jesus is the Christ even when I face obstacles. I want my lips to praise you as long as I live. Amen.*

## Song from Psalm 63

O God, you are my God; earnestly I seek you.
My soul thirsts for you;
My body longs for you in a dry and weary land.
I have seen you and beheld your power and glory.
Your love is better than life.
My lips shall praise you as long as I live.
In your name I lift my hands; at last I'm satisfied.
I think of you at night because you are my help.
I sing in the shadow of your wings.
My soul clings to you; your hand upholds me.
I will rejoice in God and praise Him with great joy!
My lips shall praise you as long as I live.

# JOURNAL YOUR SPIRITUAL WALK

During a period of my life when I was ill for months, there were days I found it difficult to pray and felt that God had deserted me. One day I knelt beside my bed with pen and paper and said, "I am staying here until I get some answers." As I waited, God began to speak to me, and I wrote. I still have those notes more than 20 years later. I hadn't heard of journaling or keeping a prayer diary at that time, but in my desperation to hear from God, that's what I did.

I wanted my prayers to be more than routine, so I began to write letters and notes to God each day expressing my emotions, my struggles, my praises, and writing down His answers through Scripture, devotional readings, and prayer. It revolutionized my prayer life and my ability to face changes and hurts that came my way.

Since then I have read books and attended seminars on journaling and want to share with you some of the benefits of journaling and some guidelines to help you get started.

- Journaling keeps you focused during your prayer and devotional time.
- Journaling creates a record of your life story and daily encounters with God.

- Journaling aids in decision-making and goal-setting.
- Journaling helps you stay in touch with your deepest feelings and serves as an emotional outlet.
- Journaling captures creativity and replenishes energy.

Here are some ideas of what to include in your journal:

- Questions you would like to ask God
- Promises from God's Word
- Song lyrics replaying in your mind
- Creative ideas
- Your feelings and emotions
- The spiritual impact of turning points in your life
- Letters to God and conversations with God
- Messages you feel God is giving you

It will be best if you develop your own plan rather than trying to copy what someone else does. Write in your journal regularly—daily if possible—but don't become a slave to it. If distracting thoughts enter your mind as you journal—such as *Call Betty* or *Buy milk*—list them in the back of your journal or on a separate sheet of paper. In a very short time you will discover that you have a book of treasures from your time with God.

## Increase Your Spiritual Awareness

During Week 1 you were encouraged to begin keeping a journal of your personal time with God. During Week 2 you were encouraged to prayerfully choose a theme for the year and to make a list of the lessons you could apply to your life from Acts 5. If you followed these suggestions, you are already on your way to recording your spiritual adventures.

Try to write in your journal every day this week. Each day make a note of the date and time of day and your location if you are away from home.

If you have not journaled before, keep your plan simple. List the names of people for whom you are praying and the scripture you read. Write a note to God giving Him thanks for what He is teaching you. Ask Him if there is anything valuable you should record.

If you are already a journaler, continue with your current plan. Record any message God gives you today through His Word and prayer. Write a short note to God thanking Him for lessons He has taught you in the past and inviting Him to expand your spiritual horizons.

At the end of the week, read all that you have written in your journal for Week 1 through Week 3.

## Scripture for This Week

(PS. 63:1-8 AND JER. 29:11-13)

Read Ps. 63:1-8 daily this week. Put a verse or two into your own words and write them in your journal each day as a prayer to the Lord.

Read Jer. 29:11-13. Write these verses in your journal and realize that God has plans for you. Remember the value of keeping a record of your walk with God.

## Praying Scripture

(PS. 63:1-4 AND JER. 29:11-13)

*Dear God,*

*I give you thanks because you are my God. Every time I think of your love for me, I long to know you better. Your power and glory have been revealed to me repeatedly. I give my future to you as I seek you with my whole heart. It is my desire to praise and glorify you as long as I live. Amen.*

## Song from Jeremiah 29:11-13

I know the plans I have for you, plans to give you hope.

Plans for your future, too.

Do not fret or worry; I will walk with you.

I am by your side.

Seek to do my will first and foremost in your life.

I will take care of you.

Give me your moments, your hours and days and weeks,

As my kingdom first you seek.

# ABSORB THE WORD

One of my friends teaches a women's Bible study at the local jail. Sometimes she asks the female inmates if they would like to read the scripture verses they are discussing. One week a professional-looking newcomer was present, and my friend Evangeline asked her if she would like to read the scripture passage from Psalms. The newcomer replied, "I don't mind reading, but I don't know how to find it; this is the very first time I've even had a Bible in my hand." The girl next to her offered to help her locate Psalms. As the newcomer read, tears came to her eyes. When she was finished, she asked if she could take the Bible to her cell so that she could read the passage again. How long has it been since a passage from the Bible has moved you this powerfully?

My husband was planning a personal prayer retreat and asked members of our congregation to give him prayer requests to take with him. One lady told me later that she asked him to pray that her hunger for God's Word would increase. A few years earlier her young daughter had died. She said that during the months following that tragedy she had felt very close to God and leaned on Him in prayer and study of His Word. However, now that life seemed to be getting easier for her, she had lost her desire for Bible reading, and her relationship with God was becoming routine. As she was telling me this, she was rejoicing that my husband's prayers and hers had been answered, and her hunger for God's Word had indeed increased. I was having a similar experience in my Bible reading and seemed more interested in reading books *about* God than studying His Word. I had recognized my lack of interest in Scripture and was determined to become more disciplined. But discipline wasn't what I really needed. I needed to hunger and thirst for God's Word. Over the years others have told me about encountering these dry spells, and admitting the need is the first step toward overcoming the problem.

Aletha Hinthorn admits in her book *How to Read the Bible So It Changes Your Life* that she hasn't always had a deep desire to read the Bible. She says:

> When we begin to allow our daily time with God to slip away, we begin to miss it less and less. In an old journal I found this entry: "I awoke and realized that because I had not been reading [the Bible] consistently, my delight and excitement with God's Word wasn't as intense. This worries me." Our desire for the Word diminishes with neglect.[1]

When Aletha Hinthorn admitted to herself that she was neglecting the Word, she was set on the path of finding a new hunger for it that has resulted in her writing several series of Bible studies. She says, "Our first step is to tell God humbly and truthfully of our desire to have fellowship with Him. Then we follow the ideas He brings."[2]

As you pray for an increased hunger for the Word and consistently read scripture seeking to hear from God, your relationship with Him will become more intimate.

## Increase Your Spiritual Awareness

Each day as you open the Bible, ask God to speak to you from His Word. As you read, regard these words as a love letter written personally to you from God. Read prayerfully with your mind engaged to hear what He has to say to you.

## Scripture for This Week

### (1 PET. 2:1-3 AND COL. 1)

Write 1 Pet. 2:1-3 in your journal.
This week ask God to make His Word fresh and alive for you.

- Read Col. 1 slowly until He begins to speak to your heart.
- Read the passage again.
- Spend a few moments meditating on the words you have just read.
- Ask God what He wants to say to you through these verses.
- Read the passage again as if God is speaking it directly to you. Then give it back to God as you understand it.
- Live with this scripture throughout the week.
- Write it on a card and read it often.
- Incorporate the verses into your daily prayers.
- Write it in your own words.
- Share it with someone else.

Continue to read the Bible daily.

## Praying Scripture

(1 PET. 2:1-5 AND COL. 1)

*Dear Lord Jesus,*

*I lay all malice, deceit, hypocrisy, envy, and evil speaking at your feet. Purify my heart. Like a newborn baby, I desire the pure milk of the Word. As I read your Word and obey, I know I will grow in my spiritual walk with you. Jesus, I have trusted you to save me by your power. I want to also trust you for each problem and allow you to reveal the hidden treasures of your wisdom. Through you my life can overflow with joy. Amen.*

### Song from Colossians 1

Christ in your hearts is the only hope of glory.
In Him lie hidden all the treasures of His wisdom.
Just as you trusted Christ to save you by His power,
Trust Him for each problem;
Let your life o'reflow with joy!

# PRAY SCRIPTURE

James 4:3 says, "When you ask, you do not receive, because you ask with wrong motives, that you may spend what you get on your pleasures." This verse demands that we ask God to alter our motives and our prayers if He has something better in mind.

But Rom. 8:26-27 reminds us that when we do not know how we should pray, the Holy Spirit makes intercession for us according to the will of God.

I have learned through the years that I can be assured I am praying God's will when I pray scripture. Not only is the Lord's Prayer a scripture prayer, but many of the Psalms are as well. Paul prayed for his Christian brothers in Col. 1. In many of Paul's writings, he tells the believers he is praying for them. We see examples of this in Phil. 1 and 1 Thess. 1 as well as other letters attributed to Paul. These are prayers we can pray for ourselves and others.

Prayerfully reading and studying scripture is a deeply life-changing way to pray. Make it a practice to keep your Bible open as you pray. God reveals many spiritual truths when we pray in this way.

## Increase Your Spiritual Awareness

This week make praying scripture your primary focus. Pray scripture daily with confidence that you are praying within the will of God.

Begin with Luke 11:2-4, the Lord's Prayer.

Next, return to Paul's prayer for believers that you studied last week in Col. 1:9-12.

Include Ps. 63 and 1 Pet. 2:1-5 from previous weeks.

It will be exciting to see where God leads you next on this prayer venture.

## Scripture for This Week

(JAMES 4)

- Prayerfully read James 4.
- Concentrate on verse 3 and ask God to reveal to you if you are asking with wrong motives.
- Pray verse 7, submitting yourself to God and resisting the devil.
- Ask God to draw you near (v. 8).
- Humble yourself before God (v. 10).
- Claim the promises in these verses.
- Read verses 11 and 12 again. Ask God to show you if you are being judgmental toward others: your pastor, your spouse, fellow Christians, coworkers, etc.

- Resolve not to participate in slander by speaking against another person or listening to gossip and judgmental words spoken against another.
- Pray that you will seek God's will today (v. 15).
- Pray that you will resist the sins of omission you are warned against in verse 17.
- Choose one verse from this chapter to commit to memory. Write it down and carry it with you and read it often until you can quote it and pray it continually.
- When someone comes to mind today, pray that he or she will submit and draw near to God. You can be assured you are praying God's will.

## Praying Scripture

(JAMES 4:7-8)

*Lord,*

*I desire to draw near to you today, to submit to you and allow you to work your will in me. I want to say no to all the devil's schemes and watch him flee when I call upon your name. Thank you that you are here. Amen.*

## Song from Luke 11:2-4

Father, may your name be honored.
May your kingdom come very soon.
Give us our food day by day, and forgive us our sins
As we forgive those who've sinned against us.
And don't let us yield to temptation.

May your kingdom come to our hearts.
This is the prayer Jesus taught His disciples
When they asked Him to teach them to pray.
Father, may your name be honored.
Will you take control of our lives?
We give you the glory, honor, and thanksgiving
Forever and ever. Amen.
Father, may your name be honored
Forever and ever.
Amen!

# SEND A PRAYER

My brother is presently serving in Iraq as a Lieutenant Colonel Chaplain in the United States Army. Many days I pray scripture for him, and at times I e-mail him that scripture prayer. I also pray scripture for other family members and friends.

Recently a family member called to share some unhappy events in his life and requested prayer for decisions being made by others regarding his future. The next morning as I was reading from Dennis Kinlaw's devotional book, *This Day with the Master,* a quote grabbed my attention:

> When a person spends enough time in the presence of God, problems begin to fade into the background and God's greatness begins to loom large. This Psalm [86] is a classic picture of the way the most serious and intense problems melt away in the presence of Almighty God, before whom they seem insignificant. As David faces God, he gets the true perspective on reality. His problems diminish and God's glory increases."[1]

I was challenged to read Ps. 86. While reading it, I began praying it, first for the one who had requested prayer the day before. Then I prayed it for myself and my brother in Iraq. I prayed that scripture many times during the week for my troubled relative. It was so powerful that I decided to mail it to him and suggested he pray it for himself.

You may wish to use this prayer for someone who is facing a time of trouble:

*Hear, O Lord, and answer my prayers for _____. He is needy. Guard his life for he is devoted to you. You are his God; save your servant who trusts in you. Have mercy on him, O Lord, for he calls on you all day long. Bring joy to _____. Help him lift up his soul to you. Thank you that you are forgiving and good, abounding in love to all who call to you. Hear his prayer and listen to his cry for mercy in this day of trouble while he is calling on you for an answer. There is no other god like you, O Lord; no deeds can compare with yours. We pray for the day when all nations you have made will come and worship before you and bring glory to your name, for you are great and do marvelous deeds. You alone are God. Teach _____ your way, and help him walk in your truth. Give him an undivided heart that he may fear your name. May he praise you as his Lord God with all his heart, and show him how to glorify your name forever. Your love is great for _____. You have delivered him from the depths. The arrogant are attacking him, and ruthless men seek his life, but you are a compassionate and gracious God. You are slow to anger but abounding in love and faithfulness. Turn to _____ and have mercy on him. Give him strength and a sign of your goodness. May his enemies be put to shame. I thank you for helping him and comforting him. Amen.*

## Increase Your Spiritual Awareness

This week I encourage you to write a scripture prayer for a friend or someone in your family and mail it to him or her with a reminder of your prayers on his or her behalf.

## Scripture for This Week

(PS. 86)

Continue to read and pray this Psalm daily.

## Praying Scripture

(PS. 86:11-13)

*Heavenly Father,*

*The prayer of the psalmist is my prayer today. Teach me your ways. I want to honor you with a pure heart and to praise you with all my heart. Your great love overwhelms me. May I give glory to your name forever! Amen.*

### Song from Psalm 86

Teach me your way, O Lord,
And I will walk in your truth.
Give me an undivided heart,
That I may honor your name.
I will praise you, O Lord, my God
With all my heart.
I want to glorify your name forever
For great is your love to me.

# WRITE A LETTER

There are various types of letters:

- Thank-you letters for gifts and services
- Bread and Butter letters as a thank-you for hospitality
- Friendly letters to keep in touch and tell what's happening in your life
- Business letters to inform or request information
- Invitations, memos, e-mail, post cards, greeting cards, love letters, etc.

When I was teaching language arts, textbooks advised students to give details and be specific in their letters. They were told that thank-you notes should name the gift and tell why they like it and how they plan to use it. Friendly letters were to include details to make the news interesting. Invitations should contain pertinent information such as what, who, where, when, and why.

There are many letters in the Bible. Several letters from Paul to churches include thanks for gifts, services, hospitality. Some extend invitations or inform that he or someone he is sending will be coming for a visit. Others are written to tell of happenings, give information, or give advice.

We sometimes think of God's Word as His letter to us. He often speaks of His love to us through His various messengers.

In Week 3 you were encouraged to write a letter to God. This is a form of prayer.

I enjoy reading Jesus' prayer in John 17. I think of it as His prayer for me because He says, "I am not praying for these alone but also for the future believers who will come to me because of the testimony of these" (v. 20, TLB). I like to read portions of that chapter as if it is a letter written directly to me.

## Increase Your Spiritual Awareness

Write a letter to God in your journal each day this week. Include any or all of the elements already named:

**Give thanks.** Be specific.

**Keep in touch.** Tell Him about what's happening in your life.

**Make your requests.**

**Invite** Him to be a part of your day.

**Add a love note.**

## Scripture for This Week

(JOHN 17 AND JOHN 14:6)

Read John 17 as if Jesus is praying it specifically for you. Turn portions of it into His letter to you telling you how He prays to the Father on your behalf.

Memorize John 14:6.

(JOHN 17:4)

*Heavenly Father,*
*    I want to follow Christ's example and bring glory to you*
*here on earth by doing everything you tell me. Amen.*

## Song from John 14:6

Jesus is the *way*—
The way to God the Father—
The way to heaven and eternal life.
Jesus is the *truth*—
And if you know the truth,
The truth through Jesus will set you free indeed!
Jesus is the *life*—
He came to give abundant life—
A joyful and victorious life.
No one comes to the Father but through Jesus.

# LISTEN WITH ANTICIPATION

One Sunday evening when Lanissa was a tiny baby and Kevin was barely four (shortly after he had prayed for Jesus to come into his heart), I was tucking him in way past his bedtime and mine. I got up very early that morning, taught Sunday School and children's church, had guests for lunch after church, did a Bible study with a couple of new Christians in the afternoon, went to a special choir practice (taking my babies with me), came home from the evening service, fed Lanissa and put her to bed, fed my husband and son, and in between, I tried to wash the lunch dishes but still hadn't finished.

When I went into the bedroom to tuck Kevin in, he asked me to read a Bible story. My reply was, "My throat's too sore."

After we both prayed, he pulled my face down to his, hugged me tightly, and said, "I love you, Mommy. Let's talk."

I pulled away and said, "I can't; I have to finish washing dishes."

Then he said, "When can we talk?"

"Maybe tomorrow," I said. I turned off the light, finished washing the dishes, and fell into bed after midnight—bone weary.

In the wee hours the next morning, I was awakened with that short conversation ringing in my ears. I began to wonder how long he may have been waiting just to talk to Mommy. Maybe tomorrow he would assume I was still too busy, or suppose by some tragedy there would be no chance to talk tomorrow. What if God answered me that way when I was in a time of dire need? For three early morning hours I lay awake learning a very difficult but welcome lesson. Oh, the value of taking time to talk—or even just to listen!

I suspect, on that night long ago, that Kevin had some things on his little heart that he wanted to share with Mommy. I am also quite sure there have been times in the past when God has had things on His big heart that He wanted to convey to me, His daughter, but I have been too busy to hear Him—busy with Christian activities, enriching projects, good things. No matter how noble the plans I make, if they cause me to be too busy to talk to God and listen to what He has to say to me, I am *way* too busy! I wonder how often I have missed Him whispering, "Let's talk."

Although I have had devotional times since childhood and have journaled during prayer for many years, I have discovered through reading those written prayers that I have done more talking than listening. A few years ago I challenged myself to listen to God for 10 minutes without interrupting Him. I have continued that practice since and have made some amazing discoveries. As you may have guessed, listening is my challenge to you this week.

## Increase Your Spiritual Awareness

Set a timer each day to listen for 10 minutes or just five minutes if 10 seems like an eternity.

Wait quietly for a moment in God's presence. Let Him calm your heart and mind. Tell Him you are going to listen to what He has to say to you today, and then listen without giving Him any requests. Write down what He says to you. He may speak a verse of scripture to you or impress on your mind the words of a song. Perhaps He will bring to mind a person who needs a word of encouragement. He may give you a word of comfort or challenge. He may ask you to join Him in some activity. Write it all down. Maybe He will say nothing. If this is the case, sit quietly in His presence and soak in His love and grace.

After your listening time:

- Give Him thanks for His love and grace and for any words He has spoken to you.
- Pray for the individuals He placed in your thoughts.
- Commit to Him your obedience for any assignment He may have given you.
- Ask God to purge your heart and conscience.
- Pray a prayer of repentance if He pointed out something that should not be in your life.

Practice this discipline daily in your personal prayer life.

## Scripture for This Week

(PS. 46)

Read Ps. 46:10 in several translations.

"Be silent, and know that I am God" (KJV and NIV).

"Stand silent! Know that I am God" (TLB).

"Cease striving" (NASB).

"Step out of the traffic! Take a long, loving look at me, your High God" (TM).

Choose your favorite version of Ps. 46:10 and memorize it. Repeat it often.

## Praying Scripture

(PS. 46:1, 10)

*O God,*

   *It is so hard for me to be still! Even when there is quietness around me, my motor can be running inside. I want to be silent on the inside, to pause awhile and know with certainty that you are God and that you, Almighty God, are with me! Thank you that you are my refuge and strength, an ever present help in trouble. Thank you for your presence with me today. Keep me calm in the hubbub of my world. Amen.*

## Song from Psalm 46

Be still and know that I am God.
Cease striving, quiet your heart to hear my voice.
I am your refuge, your strength
An ever present help in trouble.
Be still and know that I am God.

# CAPTURE DISTRACTIONS

Have you ever been praying and suddenly found yourself cleaning out the garage or a closet and wondering how you got from prayer to there? Or during your prayer time, has your mind wandered to your own agenda or family who is far away or your Christmas gift list? Did you find this especially true when you were doing your listening times last week?

What do you do to stay focused during prayer? Do you find that journaling helps?

Some of the following ideas may help you turn your unavoidable distractions into prayer.

## Distractions

*A plane is flying overhead*: Pray for the pilot and copilot to be alert. Pray for the safety and salvation of passengers. Pray that each one will hear God's appeal and respond with obedience.

*Phone interruptions*: Pray for the caller over the phone.

*Doorbell*: Ask the person at the door how you can pray for him or her.

*Neighbor's barking dog*: Pray for your neighbor. If he or she is not a Christian, pray for his or her salvation. If your neighbor is a

Christian, pray that he or she will grow spiritually. After praying for that neighbor, move to other families in your neighborhood. Ask God what He wants you to do to minister in your neighborhood.

## Wandering Thoughts

*All you have to do today:* When your thoughts wander away from your prayers to today's agenda, pray over your agenda.

*Your children:* If your mind wanders to your children, pray for your children, their teachers if your children are still in school, those who will influence their lives, their spouses or future spouses.

Remember, the enemy wants to keep you from prayer. He will divert your thoughts, cause you to doubt, and speak false ideas to you. When you hear in your mind words like: *This is a waste of time,* or *You are fooling yourself; God doesn't hear your prayers,* you can be sure these words do not come from God. Resist them with prayer. Confess your doubts to God, and ask Him to enlarge your faith. Resist the enemy; tell him that he is defeated, and that you will continue to pray even when you do not see immediate results. When Satan tells you that God does not hear or answer prayer, remind him and yourself of recent answers to prayer. Make a list of answers.

## Increase Your Spiritual Awareness

Continue your 10-minute listening times daily. I get up 10 minutes earlier in the morning to avoid distractions. If you are not a morning person, try splashing some water on your face and walking to a quiet place away from the bedroom for this sacred visit with God. Find an uncluttered place for your prayer and listening time that is as free from distractions as possible. Turn off the television and radio. You may want to silence the ringer on your phone. Allow God to calm the voices that are clamoring for your attention. Acknowledge His presence.

This week work diligently at turning your distractions into prayer. Apply some of the suggestions given above and ask God to give you some creative ways to stay focused.

## Scripture for This Week

(2 COR. 10:3-5 AND PHIL. 4:8)

Spend time this week meditating on 2 Cor. 10:3-5. As you work at handling distractions and wandering thoughts, "take captive every thought to make it obedient to Christ."

Follow the advice of Paul in Phil. 4:8 that clearly lists the things we are to think upon as we replace defeating thoughts.

You will begin to see your thought life transformed as you apply these scriptures.

Review Ps. 139:1-2 and 139:23-24.

## Scripture for This Week

(PHIL. 4:8)

*Almighty Father,*

*Teach me to turn my thoughts to wholesome things today. I want to think about true, good, noble, lovely things. I desire that my thoughts be pure. May my thoughts be admirable and praiseworthy to you, my God, my Redeemer. Amen.*

## Song from Philippians 4:8

Whatsoever things are true,
Whatsoever things are good,
I will think upon those things.
Whatsoever things are right,
Noble, lovely, pure, and bright,
I will think upon those things.
If anything is excellent, admirable, praiseworthy,
I will think upon those things.

# REVISE YOUR TO-DO LIST

I was prompted to start my 10-minute listening times by a suggestion in a book I read. I had finished the book on Saturday and shared some ideas I discovered in it with friends at lunch on Sunday. On Monday morning I resolved to give it a try to see if I could stay focused and truly listen for 10 minutes. I really did not know what to expect. I had prayed and dialogued with God in the past, and although I had listened for answers and recorded them in my journal, I had never actually timed how long I listened.

That Monday morning I set my alarm early. I was already committed to giving the first hour of my day to God. Now I was re-solved to give at least the first 10 minutes to listening to what He had to say to me. I went to the kitchen, set the timer on the stove, and sat down at the breakfast table with my spiral notebook and a pen. Almost immediately I began to write. That first entry was more like a to-do list, but it was not like any to-do list I had ever written:

Write Stormie.

Call piano tuner.

Be transparent.

Listen when Curtis calls.

Don't get bound by agenda.

Continue Stormie's prayers.

Read entire Book of Daniel.

Call Monda and Jan.

Continue timed listening and Jesus Film prayers . . .

The timer buzzed after 10 minutes. As I read what I had written, I knew this was no ordinary list. I wondered where these names and ideas originated. I knew they were from God, and I was to act on every one.

As I went through the day and followed through on my list, I began to realize that this to-do list had eternal dimensions.

I read the Book of Daniel more carefully than I had ever read scripture before, all the while praying and asking God what He wanted to teach me or reveal to me through His Word.

I called the church to get the number of a piano tuner. That is a story I will leave for later.

I did not have Stormie's address; therefore, I sent the letter via the publisher of one of her books. Her reply revealed that she had been seriously ill and enlightened me on some ways I could pray for her.

To reach Jan, a friend from my past, I first had to call my dear friend Monda to locate Jan's phone number. We had all moved so many times that Jan and I had lost track of each other. I was in the middle of a project when I was prompted to call Monda. I knew I was to stop immediately and follow through with that impulse. I also knew that it was unlikely I would find Monda at home since she travels extensively. However, she answered the phone even though she was just walking out the door. She did not have Jan's number but thought her husband, Bob, might have it. Since he was already in the car, I had to wait for them to locate the number. Monda said that Jan had been on her mind the day before during the worship service. After my call to Monda, I immediately called Jan and found her at home also. She exclaimed, "Oh, Patsy, my long-lost friend!" Jan went on to share some of the trauma she was facing with illness and other issues.

Yes, this was like no other to-do list I had ever made. The day took a totally different direction, but it was life-changing for me and for others.

After a few days, my listening times took on a different format and no longer looked like a to-do list. However, I advise making a to-do list prayerfully as you organize your day. You will find that your activities are more far-reaching and your time and energies are more effectively directed. The important thing is to obey every directive. God will give you the strength for the tasks He endorses.

## Increase Your Spiritual Awareness

Continue your listening times. You can be sure that God's words to you will always be in agreement with His Word! Remember, even if you hear nothing, there is value in sitting quietly in His presence. Breathe in His peace. Draw on His strength.

Pray as you organize your day. Let Him help you make your to-do list.

## Scripture for This Week

(JAMES 1)

Day 1: Read and meditate on verses 1-5.
Day 2: Read and meditate on verses 5-8.
Day 3: Read and meditate on verses 12-15; read 5-6 again.

Day 4: Read and meditate on verses 16-18.

Day 5: Read and meditate on verses 19-25.

Day 6: Read and meditate on verses 26-27; read 5-6 again.

Day 7: Read the entire chapter of James 1 again.

Concentrate on James 1:5 and memorize it. "If any of you lacks wisdom, he should ask God, who gives generously to all without finding fault, and it will be given to him."

## Praying Scripture

(JAMES 1:5, 17-22)

*Dear God,*

*I want to be quick to listen, slow to speak, and slow to be angry. I desire not only to listen but also to be obedient when I need wisdom and ask you what you want me to do. It amazes me that you have created me as your choice possession and that you willingly give wisdom when I come to you with my requests. It's true that everything good and perfect comes from you. Thank you! Amen.*

## Song from James 1:5

If you lack wisdom, ask of God,
And it will be given to you.
Ask in faith, expecting Him to answer,
And He will gladly give you wisdom.

# MAKE A
# JOYFUL NOISE

Several years ago I used a daily devotional guide especially pre-pared for the season between Easter and Pentecost Sunday. One day the question was asked, "If you were to write a song to God, what would be some things for which you would give Him thanks?" Next, the book suggested that the reader write a song. My mental re-sponse was: *I'm not going to do this. I'm not a song writer. It taxes my brain to even think of attempting such a thing. I marvel at how people come up with beautiful lyrics and melodies. Not only do I not write songs, I don't even write poetry. I teach my students to write award-winning poetry by exposing them to good writers, but I do not write poetry. God knows I am thankful, but I cannot write a song or a poem.*

After making the decision to bypass that directive, I moved forward in the devotional guide. It took me to Rev. 2:17, and I be-gan to wonder, *If God were giving me a new name, what would it be?* Although it was just a curious thought, before I reached the end of the chapter, I knew my new name. This was exciting to me!

"Let everyone who can hear, listen to what the Spirit is saying to the churches: Every one who is victorious shall eat of the hidden manna, the secret nourishment from heaven; and I will give to each a white stone, and on the stone will be engraved a new name that no one else knows except the one receiving it" (Rev. 2:17, TLB).

"To every one who overcomes—who to the very end keeps on doing things that please me—I will give power over the nations" (Rev. 2:26, TLB).

"And I will give you the Morning Star! Let all who can hear, listen to what the Spirit says to the churches" (Rev. 2:28-29, TLB).

The devotional next suggested scripture found in 2 Pet. 1. The entire chapter was great, but when I reached verse 19, I found myself turning the scripture into a prayer, and I began writing it.

"So we have seen and proved that what the prophets said came true. You will do well to pay close attention to everything they have written, for, like lights shining into dark corners, their words help us to understand many things that otherwise would be dark and difficult. But when you consider the wonderful truth of the prophets' words, then the light will dawn in your souls and Christ the Morning Star will shine in your hearts" (2 Pet. 1:19, TLB).

God responded to that prayer, addressing me by my new name. I proceeded to write another verse to my prayer, and He responded. I continued this dialogue with God, realizing to my amazement that I was writing a song, or at least a prayer in the form of a poem. When I was finished, I moved from the bedroom to the piano in the living room. Although no melody was in my mind, I sat down and began to sing my song and play a melody not remotely similar to anything I had heard before. This became my private prayer song to sing every day to God.

Since that day, I sing more songs to God in my private devotional times. Just as my song was a prayer, many songs contain prayerful expressions. I invite you to make music a part of your daily praise and prayer times. Even if you feel you don't have a melodious voice, you can make a joyful noise as the hymn writer in Ps. 100 suggests.

## Increase Your Spiritual Awareness

Listen to uplifting music this week.

Purchase a new CD to play as you drive.

Sit quietly and listen to at least one song each day. Absorb the words. Replay the song and sing along.

If you do not have a hymnal or book of Christian songs, try to get one. Maybe you can borrow one from your church. Read the words of one hymn each day and sing or make a joyful noise unto the Lord.

Ask yourself the same question that appeared in my devotional guide: If you were writing a song to God, what are some things for which you would give Him thanks? Sing your thanks to Him.

## Scripture for This Week

(PS. 119:54 AND PS. 100)

Meditate on Ps. 119:54.

Read Ps. 100 daily and try to memorize it. Did you memorize this as a child? If so, you may still remember it.

The song for this week was written word-for-word from Ps. 100, NIV, to help children memorize that chapter.

## Praying Scripture

(PS. 100)

*Lord God,*

*You fill my heart with joy. I want to worship you with gladness, to come before you with joyful songs, to know that you are my Creator God, and I belong to you. It seems strange to think of myself as a sheep, but I truly do need a loving shepherd to guide me. I am grateful that I can be called a sheep of your pastures! I praise your name and thank you for your goodness, love, and faithfulness. Amen.*

## Song from Psalm 100

Shout for joy to the LORD, all the earth.
Worship the LORD with gladness;
come before him with joyful songs.
Know that the LORD is God.
It is he who made us,
And we are his;
We are his people,
The sheep of his pasture.
Enter his gates with thanksgiving
And his courts with praise;
Give thanks to him
And praise his name.
For the LORD is good
And his love endures forever;
His faithfulness continues through all generations.

# SING TO
# THE LORD

We had lived in Traverse City more than three years and had not had the piano tuned since the move. The sustaining pedal was not working properly, which made the playing choppy and disconnected. For these reasons, and because of a busy schedule that involved a great deal of travel, I had not sat down at the piano for weeks.

I am by no means an accomplished pianist. I probably have less than nine months of lessons from three teachers scattered over a period of at least seven years. However, I enjoy playing and singing at home for my own pleasure and have owned my Story and Clark console piano since seminary days. This broken-pedaled, out-of-tune piano looks like new even after at least a dozen moves and after spending several months in storage two different times. The sadly silent piano had not made a joyful noise for many days when I wrote "Call the piano tuner" during my first 10-minute listening time on July 31, 2000.

Later that morning I called the church secretary to get the number of the piano tuner the church used. I gave him a call, and he said he had time available the next day. When he arrived Tuesday, his visit was shortened when he immediately found a crack in the soundboard. He removed it to take it to his shop for repair and promised to return Thursday at 1:00 P.M.

As I was listening for God to speak to me Thursday morning, I found myself writing these words: "Play my song when the piano tuner leaves. I am going to give you a new one." I knew He was referring to the song I had written two years earlier, which was the only song I had written.

I had not sung that song for many months and had forgotten some of the words. I rummaged through my bedside drawer to find the journal in which I had written the lyrics. As soon as the piano tuner drove away, I played and sang my song from 2 Pet. 1:19.

The next morning during my listening time, I made the following list as God spoke to my heart:

Listen for my new song.

Sing songs of praise.

Give tomorrow totally to me.

Listen through Scripture.

Listen now.

I hadn't been listening the full 10 minutes, but I walked from the kitchen to the bedroom to get my Bible. Listening as I moved, I wondered, *Where am I to read? Will the new song come from the Book of Daniel? (I had just finished reading Daniel.) Will it come from Hosea? (I was reading Hosea at the time.)* As I carried the Bible back to the kitchen, I saw that the bookmark was near the end of the Bible. I pulled the ribbon through and opened to Eph. 3. When I got to verse 12, I knew that was where the song would begin. As I continued to read, the words flowed, and I wrote furiously. When I finished, I looked at the clock. I had been listening for more than an hour. I had a doctor's appointment shortly and still needed to shower, dress, and drive to the office. I wondered if I would have a melody when I sat down at the piano later. No melodies were running through my mind, but the words had burned their way into my heart. Amazingly, a melody came quickly later that morning as I sat at the keyboard.

The next day I decided to see what Eph. 4 had to say since Eph. 3 had been so powerful. Before I had finished reading, God had given me a song from that chapter. On Sunday I decided to read Eph. 2, and again God gave me a song. Monday I received a song from Eph. 1; Tuesday, Eph. 5; and Wednesday, Eph. 6. Each day the song came as I prayerfully read the scripture, and the melody came when I sat down at the piano.

The songs continued to come, one or more daily, for weeks. Eventually the songs didn't come every day, but before Christmas there were more than 150. By the following Christmas, there were more than 200, and the songs continue to come occasionally even now.

My purpose in sharing that story with you is to say that this was a gift I never requested. It came to me unexpectedly as a result of my first day of 10-minute listening when God said to call the piano tuner. I had a desire to memorize more scripture and to pray scripture, and I had expressed that desire to God. My prayer was surprisingly met as God gave me the songs.

Do you suppose God has a treasure waiting for you as you listen and obey?

## Increase Your Spiritual Awareness

Continue listening each day. Read your 10-minute listening notes from Week 8 through Week 11. Have you done everything you felt God impressed you to do?

Continue singing every day. Hum or whistle if you feel you can't sing. At least speak the words aloud as if reading a sacred poem.

If you play an instrument, use it this week to praise and glorify God. Perhaps God has a song or poem or story for you to write. Maybe He has something entirely different in mind for you to do to bring praise to Him.

## Scripture for This Week

(EPH. 3)

Read and meditate on Eph. 3 this week. Read Eph. 3:12-21 every day.

## Praying Scripture

(EPH. 3:12-20)

*Dear Jesus,*

*I am awed to think that I can come without fear into your presence and be assured that you gladly welcome me each time I draw near to you. Give me strength today from your glorious riches. Fill me with your Holy Spirit and, by your power, work within me. I treasure your gift of love that surpasses knowledge. To you be glory and praise forever! Amen.*

### Song from Ephesians 3:12-21

I come fearlessly today into God's presence
Assured of His glad welcome when I pray.
As I think of the scope of His great love for me,

I fall down on my knees and boldly say:
"Out of your glorious unlimited resources
Give your mighty, inner strengthening today.
O, Holy Spirit, fill my heart with your great love divine;
May my roots grow down deep in you always."

"My love is long enough to reach past your present;
It's long enough to fill your future too.
My love is wide enough to wrap my arms of mercy
Around everyone who means so much to you.
My love is deep enough to pardon every sin and wrong,
Yet high enough to bring you home to me;
This love is great enough that you will never see the end
Or fully understand it, my dear friend.
I am able to do more than you could fathom,
More than you dare ask or even dream;
I am infinitely far beyond your highest prayers
Your highest thoughts, desires, and hopes, and means."

To you be glory, praise, and thanks forever
    For this treasured gift of your true love.
I pray that Christ himself will dwell forever here
    In my heart while strengthening from above.
Now glory be to God whose mighty power
    Is at work within me today.
I am yours forever; take and use me.
    My heart is open, you're my truth, the way!

# CELEBRATE DAILY

I was intrigued by the title of Byrd Baylor's book, *I'm in Charge of Celebrations*, so I bought the book. It's about a girl who lives in the desert. She begins by saying that sometimes people ask her if she is lonely out there with the desert all around her. Her response makes me chuckle: "Lonely? I can't help laughing when they ask me that. I always look at them . . . surprised. And I say, 'How could I be lonely? I'm the one in charge of celebrations.'"[1] She continues to say that last year she gave herself 108 celebrations besides the ones they close school for. She keeps a notebook, records the date, then writes about the celebration. She says, "You can tell what's worth a celebration because your heart will pound and you'll feel like you're standing on top of a mountain and you'll catch your breath like you were breathing some new kind of air."[2]

This unnamed girl has a Rainbow Celebration Day and a Green Cloud Day. One of her greatest celebrations is called The Time of Falling Stars. Her New Year Celebration comes in the spring.

Although I don't live in the desert and have only visited the desert a couple of times, I can relate to this girl. I, too, have come to realize that I am in charge of celebrations in my life. I first realized it during the Lenten season a few years ago. I was praying for a plan to make the weeks leading up to Easter significant in my spiritual life. In the past, I had denied myself something during this time; some years I gave up a certain food or some enjoyable activity to remind me of all Christ gave up to come and dwell on Earth and give His life for my sins. Other years I made a point to extend Christ's love to someone each day or to fast a meal or a portion of a meal. The year before, my plan had been to spend the first hour of the day in prayer. However, this particular year, in response to my request for a way to personally prepare for Easter, God gave me the idea of finding a way to celebrate each day from Ash Wednesday until Easter Sunday, the Resurrection Celebration!

If you are unfamiliar with the purpose of Lent, it is explained in the book, *This Day—A Wesleyan Way of Prayer*, as follows:

> Lent began as a time of final intense preparation for those adults who were to be baptized at Easter and as a time of renewed spiritual intensity among all who had previously been baptized. In imitation of Jesus' sojourn of forty days and nights in the desert, it came to be a season of forty fast days. Sundays were excluded since the Lord's Day, being a perpetual commemoration of the joy of his victory over death, can never be a fast day. Therefore, Lent begins on a Wednesday, named for the ashes placed on the foreheads of the faithful both as a sign of repentance and as a reminder that we have come from dust and will return to dust. Therefore, Lent is a journey from death to resurrection; from the natural death we have earned through our sins to the gift of life we can never merit but which God nevertheless offers us in Christ who dies for us and with us, who joins us to himself in his victory over death.[3]

It wasn't hard to think of ways to celebrate each day:

- Celebration of Christ risen

- Celebration of forgiveness of sins and salvation

- Celebration of eternal life

- Celebration of God's love

- Celebration of friendship

Like the desert child, I had a notebook and made a list of my celebrations. Some days I watched a sunrise or sunset and celebrated. I celebrated a rainbow day when I saw rainbows both in the early morning and double rainbows at sunset. They were something to behold! I walked along Grand Traverse Bay and celebrated. I read the Easter story and celebrated. I celebrated with a picnic in the park and by enjoying an ice cream cone. I learned to celebrate at unusual times and in surprising places. My life has never been the same.

Like a child, I get excited about sunrises and rainbows, the fragrance of a burning candle and the aroma of a delicious meal. My heart is filled with gratitude when I experience God's blessings. However, I think one of my most significant celebrations came a few months ago during my devotional time. The sermon I had heard the night before encouraged us to celebrate the goodness of God. The next morning I was alone at my kitchen table looking through the windows of my breakfast room at God's beautiful world. I lit a fragrant candle to add a special touch to my listening and prayer time. The idea came to allow the Holy Spirit to prepare a table before me and as my priest to serve me the bread and wine signifying Christ's broken body and shed blood. I chose a beautiful crystal goblet for the grape juice and a lovely china plate for the bread. I read the Scripture account of the Lord's Supper with His disciples and partook of the bread as His Spirit spoke the words: "Take and eat. This is my body." Next, I gave thanks as I took the cup remembering His words: "This is my blood of the covenant which is poured out for many." It was a very sacred, unforgettable celebration for me. I get emotional retelling it here.

You are in charge of the celebrations in your life. Have you become so burdened that you have forgotten to celebrate? Jesus knew how; He can teach you.

## Increase Your Spiritual Awareness

Find a way to celebrate each day this week.

- Celebrate a sunrise or sunset.
- Celebrate sitting quietly in a park or by a stream of water.
- Return to the site of your salvation or sanctification or a recent spiritual renewal and celebrate.
- Kneel at the altar of your church and celebrate.
- Read the Easter story and celebrate.
- Participate in the Holy Sacrament and celebrate.
- Sing and celebrate.

## Scripture for This Week

(MARK 14:1-26; PS. 145; AND LEV. 23)

Day 1: Read Mark 14:1-9. How did this woman with the beautiful flask of perfume celebrate?

Day 2: Read Mark 14:12-16. Pay careful attention to how the disciples obeyed Jesus' instructions in preparing for the Passover. Meditate on how you can prepare your heart for His words to you.

Day 3: Read Mark 14:17-25. Reflect on your most recent participation in the Sacrament of the Lord's Supper.

Day 4: Read Mark 14:26. Sing a hymn of praise.

Day 5: Read Mark 14:1-26 again.

Day 6: Read Lev. 23. Read Lev. 23:1-8 again and reflect.

Day 7: Read Psalm 145 aloud and celebrate!

## Praying Scripture

(LEV. 23)

*Dear God,*

*In Leviticus you spoke to Moses and appointed a number of feasts to be observed as sacred assemblies and celebrations. I can see that the feasts you proclaimed were to be joyous occasions celebrating past acts of God while giving hope for the future. I want to celebrate your work in my life and the hope I have for the future. Thank you for the gift of salvation and for salvation history that weaves its way throughout the pages of the Old Testament into the New Testament in the life of Jesus and His followers. I count it a high privilege to be among His followers and celebrate daily His work in my life. Amen.*

## Song from Psalm 145

I will praise you my God and King!

I will bless your name each day and forever.

Great is Jehovah, greatly praise him.

His greatness is beyond discovery.

Let each generation tell its children

What glorious things he does.

I will meditate about your glory,

Splendor, majesty, and miracles.
Your awe-inspiring deeds shall be on every tongue.
I will proclaim your greatness.
Everyone will tell about how good you are
And sing about your righteousness.
Jehovah is kind and merciful,
Slow to get angry, full of love.
He is good to everyone, His compassion
Intertwined with everything He does.
All living things shall thank you, Lord,
Your people will bless you;
They will talk about your kingdom
And mention examples of your power.
They will tell about your miracles.
The Lord lifts the fallen and those bent beneath their loads.
The eyes of all humankind look to you for help.
You give them their food as they need it.
You satisfy the hunger and the thirst of living things.
The Lord is fair in everything He does.
He is full of kindness, close to all who call on Him.
He fulfills the desires of those who trust in Him.
He hears their cries for help and rescues them.
I will praise my God and King
And bless His holy name forever.

# DE-CLUTTER
# YOUR HOME

Earlier this week my husband cleaned out his closet and drawers and gathered items to take to a compassionate ministries center. A few months earlier, I took a carload of stuff—good stuff —to another ministry in our city. As I sorted through closets and shelves, I kept telling myself, *Let it go; I don't need or use all this. Someone else can use it.* These weren't overused, shabby things; they were in good condition. I simply had more than enough and wanted to share with those who didn't have quite enough.

Simplifying and de-cluttering my home is exhilarating to me.

Although this particular cleaning mania happened in the spring, my impulse to sort and remove can kick-in anytime of the year! I smile when I think of a friend's comment: "When I don't get my spring cleaning done, I call it fall cleaning. If I don't get it done in the fall; well, I'm back to spring cleaning." I got the message. Sometimes it just doesn't get done, and dust and clutter accumulates. Another friend suggests cleaning one room per month, and the whole idea isn't so overwhelming.

Recently, I was looking for an important paper in a file cabinet I rarely open. Even though it was early in the morning, I began tossing items such as outdated pictures and bulletin board ideas from long-ago teaching days, clutter that had accumulated in hidden places.

There is another kind of housecleaning I recommend: spiritual "spring cleaning." This is a time to prayerfully go through your home and rid it of belongings that do not enhance your Christian life.

Read Deut. 7:26. "Do not bring a detestable thing into your house or you, like it, will be set apart for destruction."

Pray over your home as you do a spiritual clean-up. Stormie Omartian's book, *Lord, I Want to Be Whole*, suggests the following things be destroyed:

- Reading material that deals with the occult
- Paintings or artifacts that exalt other gods
- Tapes, CDs, DVDs, and computer games that are negative or satanic
- Clothes that do not glorify God
- Anything depicting immorality
- T-shirts with a sexual innuendo or alcohol advertisement
- Reminders of past marriages, old sweethearts, unhappy relationships

"In fact, anything you possess that reminds you of people, incidents, or things that are not of the Lord (or make you react negatively with depression, anger, anxiety, or fear) must be eliminated. Give them away if they are useful to someone who has no emotional tie to them."[1]

Stormie continues: "What about your computer? Do you have access to pornographic or other questionable sites? What we put into our minds through the Internet stays there and influences our lives, no matter how fleeting or harmless it may seem."[2]

She gives advice on how to use discernment. "Fill your heart and mind with God's Word. Spend much time in prayer and worship. Then ask, 'Lord, show me if there is anything detestable in my house.' Go through your closets and cupboards. Check your walls and bookshelves. Throw out anything suspicious. Things that don't *build* you should not be part of your life."[3]

While you are doing your spiritual housecleaning, you might find items to donate to charity. You, too, may decide you don't need all your clothes, dishes, and linens that others may find useful. This is the week to begin decluttering your home. Start with one drawer or closet. Eventually it will get done.

## Increase Your Spiritual Awareness

Take a prayer walk through your home to look for items that should be removed. You can use the list above as a guide. If there is a question, let it go. Pray over every room of your home and ask God to fill the empty spaces with His presence and peace.

As you walk through your home:

- Give thanks for the gifts and treasures you find there.
- Pray blessings on each person you see in pictures or each person who comes to mind when you encounter a gift they have given.
- Ask God to permeate each room with His Spirit.
- Remove ungodly books, pictures, videos, magazines, etc.
- Seek God's direction for other ways to pray.

## Scripture for This Week

(PS. 101)

Focus on verses 1-4. If possible, read these verses from two or three different translations and prayerfully consider how these verses might impact what you have in your home.

## Praying Scripture

(PS. 101:1-4)

*Dear God,*

*It is easy to sing of your love and to praise you when I am careful to live a blameless life. I want to lead a life of integrity in my home. I choose not to read or watch things that are ungodly. I will carefully guard what I allow to come into my life. I want to stand in your presence with a pure heart. Amen.*

### Song from Psalm 101:1-4

I will sing about your loving kindness, Lord.
I will try to walk a blameless path.
I will set no wicked thing before my eyes.
Help me to walk within my home with a perfect heart.

# REMOVE THE BAGGAGE

The first day of school my aunt and mother took my cousin and me to our classroom to meet the teacher. The teacher greeted us at the door and asked us to find a chair that fit us. My cousin and I were seated across the table from each other when we were given a worksheet and told to find the matching letters. The assignment seemed simple until I came to the capital *M* and *W*. While thinking about what to do with that pair, I kept telling myself they were the same although one was upside down, and I wondered if the teacher would call that the same or different. My five-year-old mind wrested with that awhile, finally made a decision, and then didn't know how to change it even if I wanted to because we were using crayons. I discovered I had made the wrong choice when my paper was returned with a big red circle around the *M* and the *W*. My cousin hadn't made the same mistake. She had a star! Although I never said the words out loud, I said to myself, *I must not be smart.* I was stuck on that mistake. I felt I couldn't measure up, and I compared myself to my cousin who made a perfect score. My first report card reinforced that belief. I had a couple of Bs; my cousin had all As. My older sister also had all As. The entire year I could never get higher than a B in handwriting. Emotional baggage began to collect.

The following school year I noticed that the teacher had written my name in a new, hardback reader. I told myself, *Since I can write my name. I believe I'll rewrite it.* I carefully and proudly erased her handwriting and wrote my own name. I didn't show it to anyone but felt a sense of accomplishment even though I knew my writing wasn't quite as neat as the teacher's. The books were collected with no one discovering my secret, but the next time the books were distributed by the teacher, she unhappily observed my workmanship. I was humiliated when she showed what I had done to the whole the class. She ordered me to sit under her desk for punishment. I sat there confused but unremorseful. *What had I done wrong? Wasn't it important that I knew how to write my name?* I hadn't been deliberately disobedient. I couldn't remember anyone telling me not to write my name in the book. I was hurt and uncertain and felt I couldn't do anything right. More baggage.

I recall going to a family reunion when I was about seven or eight. I was usually one of the youngest children at these family gatherings, but one of my dad's relatives had brought a friend with her who had a child who was a year or two younger than I. There was no one else there her age, and she seemed very unhappy. I knew all the good places to play at my grandmother's farm, so—shy I as was—I decided to try and make friends with her. I had seen my father and other adults gently pinch the cheek of a child and say something like, "Hello there, honey." I decided that might be a nice, friendly gesture. We stood on the front porch staring at each other for a moment before I got the courage to make my first move. Just as I reached to pinch her cheek and say, "Hello there, honey," she went flying across the lawn pointing and screaming, "She pinched me! She pinched me!" As everyone turned in my direction, my aunt and cousin angrily hurried across to the porch to ask me if I had pinched her. I had to say yes, but I tried to explain my motive and my lack of malice. I was interrupted, not believed, and scolded publicly. For the rest of the day I felt that everyone hated me, and for years I felt that my aunt and cousin might still see me as that bratty little pincher. Years later, I asked my aunt and cousin if they remembered the incident; neither of them did. They couldn't even recall who had come to the reunion with them. Yet the baggage had lived in my heart all those years.

A minister at my daughter's church preached a powerful, visual message on what to do with the internal burdens that have accumulated through the years. As he told stories of his life and gave examples of the emotional baggage he collected through the years, one by one he added suitcases, sports bags, and pieces of luggage to his arms. Eventually he was laboring and perspiring under the load while trying to walk around the platform as he preached. Then he began to tell of the help he had received from a Christian counselor and his discovery that he had erroneously given himself negative messages and built a protective shield around himself. He then removed the baggage piece by piece as he explained that healing took place when he acknowledged the harm, worked through each incident appropriately, and lifted the burden from his own weakened heart to God. That is what we are invited to do in Ps. 55:22: "Cast your cares on the LORD and he will sustain you."

God helped me give my baggage to Him during a period of illness when my husband sent me and our baby daughter to my parents' home for rest while he cared for our son who was in school. During those days alone in bed, God began to give me insight, and I decided to go back in my memory as far as I could reach and take a prayer walk through my life. At that time I had never heard of healing memories and taking a prayer walk through my past to the present, and I didn't know anyone who had done such a thing. Today I am acquainted with Christian counselors and prayer directors who take individuals through emotional healing prayer, but at that time, in my own way, I started back at the beginning and remembered everything I could. When I came to a change point in my life—a hurt, rejection, broken relationship—I allowed God to help me work through it. I asked Him through His blessed Holy Spirit to reveal to me things He felt I should know—wrong motives, bad attitudes, denial of the real issues. I confessed and asked Him to forgive all the ugly things I saw. I gave thanks for the good memories. I allowed Him to forgive through me those persons who had brought hurt into my life—both intentional and unintentional. I can truly say, "If the Son therefore shall make you free, ye shall be free indeed" (John 8:36, KJV).

A few years later I met Lana Bateman, the founder of Philippian Ministries based in Dallas, Texas. She is a prayer director who leads people through prayer walks for inner healing and also trains prayer directors. In her book *God's Crippled Children*, she tells her story and the background for Philippian Ministries. Since I have become a part of Philippian Ministries, I have seen amazing, liberating stories unfold. We do not have to continue to carry the baggage. There is divine relief.

I have great respect for Christian counselors and psychiatrists who are skilled in using biblical principles to help persons come to wholeness. They join Christ in His mission to "bind up the brokenhearted, to proclaim freedom for the captives and release from darkness for the prisoners" (Isa. 61:1). Remember, "the truth will set you free" (John 8:32). Allow the Holy Spirit to be your counselor to bring inner healing. He may use some of His human emissaries to assist Him. His healing is no less a miracle, no matter how

He completes His work. "Cast your burden on the LORD, and He shall sustain you" (Ps. 55:22, NKJV).

## Increase Your Spiritual Awareness

This week I am asking you to once again take a prayer walk, but this time it is not through your home but through the rooms of your heart, starting with your earliest memories up to the present. This may take longer than a week, but begin the journey today. Here are a few books to help you find your way:

*Lord, I Want to Be Whole* by Stormie Omartian

*Depression Hits Every Family* by Grace Ketterman

*The Healing Journey* by Daryl E. Quick

*Released from Shame* by Sandra D. Wilson

*Telling Yourself the Truth* by William Backus and Marie Chapian

*Making Peace with Your Past* by Norman Wright

*God's Crippled Children* by Lana Bateman (Must be ordered from Philippian Ministries, 972-552-1097)

You may have memories in your past that are painful to visit, and this is a good time to acknowledge them. Talk to God about your pain. Maybe you will want to talk to your pastor, a counselor, or a trusted friend. Give God time to do His work. Express your thanks to God for His faithfulness in meeting you at your point of need.

## Scripture for This Week

(PS. 55; 2 COR. 1:3-7; PS. 30; PS. 119:165-68)

Day 1: Read Ps. 55 then return to verses 1 and 2.

Day 2: Read Ps. 55:16-19 again.

Day 3: Memorize Ps. 55:22a.

Day 4: Read 2 Cor. 1:3-7. Meditate on verse 3.

Day 5: Read 2 Cor. 1:3-7 again. Meditate on verse 4.

Day 6: Read Ps. 119:165-68 and pray this scripture.

Day 7: Read Ps. 30 and rejoice.

## Praying Scripture

### (PS. 119:165-68 AND PS. 30)

*Dear God, my counselor, my healer,*

*My life is an open book before you, O my God. I follow your instructions and abide by your counsel. I exalt you, O God. I praise your holy name. You have rescued me. I cried to you for help, and you restored my health. I wept many night hours, but you heard my desperate call and brought inner peace. You have truly turned my mourning into joy. I cannot be silent. I sing for joy and give thanks to you forever. Amen*

## Song from Psalm 119:165-68

My life's an open book before you, O my God.

I follow your instructions; how I love them.

I abide by your counsel; I do what you tell me.

My life's an open book before you, O my God.

# REMEMBER
# TO FORGET

I remember a story about a college professor who had an un-believably good memory. On the first day of class each semester, he asked each student to give his or her name. He then was able to go back around the room and repeat each student's name—regardless of the number of students in the class. He often demonstrated his memorization ability by having a large number of items named—chalkboard, chair, book, etc., and then repeating each item in order.

The story circulated one day, however, that this professor drove downtown, parked his car, and shopped awhile. When he came home on the bus, his wife asked him where the car was. He had forgotten where he parked it!

A friend of mine who usually rode the bus to work was run-ning late one day and missed the bus. He drove his car to work, parked, but, as was his usual habit, took the bus home. When he arrived home and discovered his car was gone, he called the police to report it stolen. Of course, the police found his car on the street near his workplace. Oops.

I remember a television commercial from a few years ago for a seminar that boasted it could teach individuals a memorization technique that would enable them, after the first day, to read a page from a book and recite it from memory.

A few weeks later, I took part in a program at church that included singing with a college student. I sang a solo, and then he sang a solo followed by our duet. I was then to give a memorized reading with the choir humming in the background. I finished my solo, and while Tim was singing his, I reviewed in my mind the opening words of my speech. Suddenly, I realized Tim was singing lyrics I had never heard. I had to stifle a smile because the song and the occasion were quite serious. We made it through the program, though, and at the end of the service, Tim ran across the platform and said, "I'm so sorry; I hope I didn't mess you up." He sheepishly continued, "You'd never believe I brought a book home from school to read this weekend titled *How to Improve Your Memory!*" I had to laugh out loud.

There's nothing wrong with trying to improve one's memory; in fact, it's is a good thing. However, there are some things we must remember to forget if we are to enjoy peace of mind.

The apostle Paul says in Phil. 3:13-14: "But this one thing I do, forgetting those things which are behind, and reaching forth unto those things which are before, I press toward the mark for the prize of the high calling of God in Christ Jesus" (KJV).

We all have mistakes and failures in our pasts that we must put behind us in order to move on. If the failure can be categorized as sin, which is defined in James 4:17 as knowing to do good and not doing it, it must be confessed. "If we confess our sins, he is faithful and just to forgive us our sins and to cleanse us from all unrighteousness" (1 John 1:9, KJV). Once God has forgiven, the shortcoming is removed and forgotten, and in His eyes it is as if it never happened; we are justified. Our sins are removed "as far as the east is from the west," never to be remembered against us again (Ps. 103:12). If God has forgiven you, you must also forgive *yourself* and accept His forgiveness.

Once an incident is implanted in the mind, it stays in the conscious or subconscious. When I suggest that you "forget" it, I mean deal with it; bring it to God and choose to not dwell on it by replaying it in your mind again and again. *Remember* to *forget*.

Some of our past failures are not associated with sin. Maybe you tried out for the basketball team and didn't make it. Perhaps you struggled with math or science or another subject in school, and you felt like a failure. Often we carry *false* guilt from situations that weren't really our fault, such as the divorce of parents. What do we do with these hurts?

I was haunted for years by something I did when I was in elementary school. A group of my friends convinced me to tattle on a boy for something we provoked him into doing. He and I attended different schools the next year, and soon my family moved to another part of the state. I long ago forgot his name and couldn't locate him if I tried; however, for years I struggled with this memory. I prayed for God to help me remember his name so that I could try to find him and tell him I was sorry. As of today, that has not happened. Finally, I asked God to help me deal with my feelings of regret and remorse. Here is the threefold plan He gave me, which I have used in many circumstances since:

- First, I thank God for hearing my regret and remorse for what I did. I give Him thanks for forgiving me of my wrongdoing and poor choices. I do this aloud if I am alone.

- Next, I pray blessings on this man. I pray for his salvation if he is not a Christian. I pray for his family, work, and all aspects of his life that come to my mind. I ask God to direct my prayers on his behalf.

- Finally, I purposely turn my thoughts to other things—a scripture, song, or project. I may not be able to stop all the thoughts that enter my mind, but I can control those I choose to dwell on.

Are you struggling in some area of past failure? You can bring these issues to God in prayer for forgiveness, cleansing, and restoration. It is possible that memories surfaced last week in your prayer walk that are causing you grief today. Proper confession and grieving are in order, but freedom from the bondage should follow. That is possible by accepting God's gift of forgiveness and *remembering* to *forget*, then moving on.

A seminary student met one of his professors as he returned to campus from lunch. They talked for quite awhile, and as they parted, the professor asked my friend, "Which way was I headed when we met? I can't remember if I am going to lunch or returning." Although it is valuable to remember to forget the past, it is vitally important to remember where you are headed—"toward the mark for the prize of the high calling of God in Christ Jesus" (Phil. 3:14, KJV).

## Increase Your Spiritual Awareness

Apply the threefold plan for past failures that come to your mind this week. There is no need to continue to carry false guilt—or even true guilt—over past sins that have been confessed and forgiven. Christ came to liberate you. Give Him thanks. Rejoice!

Practice forgetting. The late Dr. Chapman believed that forgetting was an art. He said:

> Yes, forgetting is an art, an art implying practices just the opposite of remembering. Repetition, exaggeration, associa-

tion, and imagination are all involved in memory methods. But if you want to forget a thing, refuse to dwell upon it, minify its importance, reduce its rank, look at it from the perspective of things that really matter, make it inconsequential, and, finally, isolate it, as the scientists do disease germs in the laboratory. Refuse to connect it with persons and motives, and positively forbid the imagination to dwell upon it. Forget it. Learn to forget by forgetting, for forgetting is an art."[1]

Review Week 11 and make a joyful noise! Remember to sing daily. You have been given heavy assignments these past three weeks. If you've been working on your baggage and de-cluttering your home, it is important to give praise and rejoice as you allow God to do His deep work in you.

## Scripture for This Week

(PHIL. 3:12-14; 1 JOHN 1; 2:1-14; 5:13-15; PS. 103:12)

Read Phil. 3:12-14 daily.

Read 1 John 1 and 1 John 2:1-14 and search your heart for unconfessed sin.

Read prayerfully 1 John 5:13-15 and Ps. 103:12.

Read Ps. 30:11-12 from last week and rejoice.

## Praying Scripture

(PS. 103:12)

*Dear Father of forgiveness,*

*You have forgiven my transgressions and removed them from me as far as the east is from the west, buried in the depths of the sea, never to be remembered against me. I am free, cleansed, purified by the blood of Jesus, redeemed, liberated. That is worth shouting from the rooftop! Thank you for placing a song in my heart! Amen.*

## Song from Psalm 103

I bless the holy name of God with all my heart.
Yes, I will bless the Lord for the glorious things He does.
He forgives all my sins. He heals my diseases.
He redeems my life from destruction.
He surrounds me with loving kindness and with tender
    mercies.
He fills my life with good things,
And my youth is renewed like the eagle's.
The Lord is merciful and He is so gracious,
Slow to anger and abounding in mercy.
For as the heavens are high above the earth,
So great is his mercy to those who fear him.
As far as the east is from the west,
So far has he removed our transgressions from us.
The loving kindness of the Lord is everlasting
To those who reverence him.
His salvation is to the children's children
Of those who obey his commandments.
The Lord has made the heavens his throne.
Let everything everywhere bless the Lord.
Bless the Lord, O My soul!

# CREATE NEW MEMORIES

I invite you to continue the Phil. 3:13-14 journey: "But this one thing I do, forgetting those things which are behind, and reaching forth unto those things which are before, I press toward the mark for the prize of the high calling of God in Christ Jesus" (KJV).

During Week 15 you began removing baggage from the past. Week 16 you began to work through the sins and failures of your past. This week the focus will be on sins committed by others that have left you with deep wounds.

Just as there is a process of healing that takes place following surgery or broken bones, there is a process involved in the healing of deep wounds and broken hearts resulting from betrayal and abuse. I realized this when I suffered a crushing blow and felt unbearable emotional pain. I wondered how I could function with this crushed spirit and deep ache in my heart. I knelt beside a chair in my bedroom and poured out my heart to God, telling Him I could not go on like that, and I asked Him to bring healing. I discovered in time that the pain was gone, and I began to try to reconstruct the steps in the healing process. I sat down at the kitchen table with a portable typewriter those many years ago and typed the following list so I could refer to it in the future:

- Even the Christian life has hurts and hard times.

- Many times we have little or no control over the hurts that come our way.

- Even though we have little or no control over them, we can control our responses to them.

- It is human to feel inward pain when we're treated unfairly.

- It is also human to dwell on our pain, relive the experience, and feel whoever inflicted the pain deserves punishment.

- It is tempting to harbor unkind thoughts against those who hurt us.

- Yielding to those temptations allows a root of bitterness to develop, resentment to fester, and bad attitudes to become a way of life.

- Positive thinking will not eliminate these feelings.

- Only God can heal our wounds and fill us with compassion and forgiveness so that we can grow in His likeness.

- We must allow God to do this; He will not do it against our will.

- If we persist in hard feelings and ill will, we hamper our availability to be used by God, and our witness is ineffective.

- What we are powerless to do for ourselves, He does for us as a result of our willingness to be healed. There is no human explanation for what takes place within the spirit as a result of this healing.

## Increase Your Spiritual Awareness

- Let the healing process begin—or continue! Give God the hurts of your past and allow Him to apply His healing touch layer by layer.
- Read the list again. Determine where you are in the process and move to the next step.
- Refer to Week 13 and plan a celebration!

## Scripture for This Week

(ROM. 8 AND PS. 30)

Read Rom. 8 daily and be comforted! Pray portions of this chapter for the one who inflicted pain. Pray it for yourself.

Read Psalm 30 and rejoice!

## Praying Scripture

(ROM. 8 AND PS. 30)

*Dear Jesus,*

*Thank you for your healing touch on the inner pain I have carried so long. I know that you are working deep in my heart in ways I cannot see. You have turned my pain into peace and my sadness into joy. You are faithful. Thank you that nothing can separate me from your love. I give you praise! Amen.*

## Song from Psalm 30:10-12

My God is faithful,

He turned my sorrow into joy.

He gave me garments of praise instead of mourning.

I cannot be silent.

I sing glad praises to the Lord.

O Lord, my God, I give thanks to you forever.

# FORGIVE FREELY

I was a young pastor's wife in my 20s working alongside my husband in our first church after graduating from seminary. There was a large group of teens in the church, and it was growing. One of my responsibilities was teen Bible quizzing. We returned late one Saturday afternoon from a quizzing tournament where we won the championship trophy. My husband was scheduled to conduct a home dedication that evening for a couple who had recently started attending our church and had found personal relationships with Christ. I attended the dedication, even though I was very tired.

The next morning after teaching Sunday School, I rushed to the sanctuary for the worship service and sank into my seat just as the music began. I was battling some throat problems, so I didn't sing in the choir that day. As the service ended, before I had an opportunity to speak to anyone, the lady in front of me turned and said, "Do you have something against me?" I was taken aback and asked why she would think such a thing. She said that she had dreamed about me the night before, and I could tell from her tone that it was not a good dream. She refused to give me any details, but she said her dreams were always true. I was dumbfounded, but

I assured her that I had no animosity toward her. It was obvious that she was not convinced.

As I started to leave, I noticed that the sanctuary was almost empty except for the mother of one of my quizzers who was waiting at the back of the church. She did not have a happy face. As I approached her, she said, "You have ruined my daughter for life!" I couldn't imagine what she was talking about. We had experienced a wonderful, exciting adventure at the quiz the day before, and I was unaware of any problem concerning her daughter. She continued to emotionally pour out her frustration because of an insignificant issue in which I felt innocent. I tried to say something helpful, but she repeated that I had ruined her daughter's life and stormed out. I ran downstairs to a vacant room where I sobbed until my husband later found me. He had gathered our infant son, Kevin, from the nursery. As we drove home, I poured out fragments of the two incidents. His first response was, "I'll go talk to each of those ladies." Even at my young age, I knew that wasn't the answer. Both of these ladies were dear to me, and they and their husbands were active leaders in our church. If we talked about it to anyone in the congregation, I could envision the situation growing out of proportion and people feeling they should take sides. I didn't want that to happen, but I needed to tell someone. And I knew who that someone was!

After lunch, I put the baby down for a nap, and Curtis went back to his office at church to work on his evening sermon so that I could be alone to pray and process. I knelt beside the sofa in our family room with a book I had recently read based on the love chapter, 1 Cor. 13, titled *To Live in Love*, by Eileen Guder. I was devastated, and I knew I had to go back to church in a few hours and face those ladies again. I was afraid I would burst into tears if accusing words were spoken to me. I needed divine help. When Curtis came home, I told him I felt we were not to discuss this with anyone, not even with each other. He agreed, and we kept that commitment. I was still praying as we drove to church. When Curtis dropped me off at the front door I could see the cars of both families in the parking lot. As I climbed the steps with a heavy heart, I prayed again, *Oh God, please help me.* I met the first lady immediately in the foyer and the second one just inside the sanctuary. I talked to both ladies and was able to enjoy the service and face other people with a joyful heart. As we drove home later I realized that I had not had even a fleeting thought of the morning's incidents since I prayed that final prayer on my way into the church two hours earlier. I knew without a doubt that God had given me a miracle. He took my hurting heart, my prayers, my willingness to forgive and release, and did His work. I continued to obey His counsel not to talk about the event or replay it in my mind. I don't remember ever praying about it again. The work was done. Interestingly, I never once recalled those hurtful confrontations when I was with those ladies on future occasions, and I saw them several times every week at church and social events. God was faithful.

God gave me His version of forgiving and forgetting. I can still recall what happened that Sunday morning, but it is without bitterness and with only peace. I have found that God works uniquely in each situation. Don't expect your forgiveness stories to be the same as mine or anyone else's. Someone may have told you that you must forgive and forget, but totally forgetting is impossible. The events of our lives can be recalled or stored in the subconscious having an effect on us emotionally, physically, and spiritually. Through God's grace, we can choose to forgive, and when the event is remembered, it can be without pain or animosity.

I cannot explain forgiveness. I am human; forgiveness is divine. Although I cannot fully comprehend forgiveness, I have experienced it. I have received it, and I have extended it. Richard Foster gives some helpful thoughts on the subject of forgiveness in his book *Prayer—Finding the Heart's True Home.* He explains what forgiveness is not:

Forgiveness does not mean that we will cease to hurt. The wounds are deep, and we may hurt for a very long time. Just because we continue to experience emotional pain does not mean that we have failed to forgive.

Forgiveness does not mean that we will forget. That would do violence to our rational faculties . . . No, we remember, but in forgiving we no longer use the memory against others.

Forgiveness is not pretending that the offense did not really matter. It did matter, and it does matter, and there is no use pretending otherwise. The offense is real, but when we forgive, the offense no longer controls our behavior. Forgiveness is not acting as if things are just the same as before the offense. We must face the fact that things will never be the same. By the grace of God they can be a thousand times better, but they will never again be the same.[1]

Richard Foster then defines forgiveness in this way:

What then is forgiveness? It is a miracle of grace. . . . Forgiveness means we will no longer use the offense to drive a wedge between us, hurting and injuring one another. . . . In forgiveness we are releasing our offenders so that they are no longer bound to us. In a very real sense we are freeing them to receive God's grace.

God has bound himself to forgive when we forgive. Perhaps you have felt deeply the load of guilt at your offense against heaven. You have been uneasy and unsure of your pardon from God. You long for some assurance that will give you peace. Well, here is assurance given by the highest authority. Jesus Christ, the eternal son, guarantees your acquittal: "If you forgive others their trespasses, your heavenly Father will also forgive you" (Matt. 6:14).[2]

Are you struggling with forgiveness? In *Key to the Loving Heart*, Karen Mains suggests that congregations should have forgiveness services, and she includes a liturgy of forgiveness. This week we will adapt her forgiveness list.

## Increase Your Spiritual Awareness

Take your time and pray specific prayers for forgiveness this week using this tool from *The Key to the Loving Heart*:

**I forgive people for all the things they haven't done:**

- For no phone calls when I was absent or in great need of spirit.
- For the lack of greeting, which seemed to be a deliberate cut.
- For not being invited into homes on hospitality nights.
- For not being included in evenings of fellowship.
- For no one caring for me as a person, but for everyone only wanting from me the things I can do for them or for this community.
- For those who have withheld love when I desperately needed love extended.

- For those who have insisted upon helping me in *their* way rather than in the way I needed help.

**I forgive the things that have been said:**

- The words, words, words, that harm me more than sticks and stones and sometimes damage me in deeper, more lasting ways.

- Pious phrases telling me how to improve myself when I thought I was really making progress in that area.

- Words traveling through third parties.

- Criticism that tore the petals off some new flower God was nurturing in the hothouse of my soul.

- Jealousy, sugar-coated in devious love, a truly bitter pill.

- Those who so blithely report what other people feel, think, and say about me, especially the negative.

- Gossip, pure and simple, aimed at me.

- People who have questioned my motives.

**I forgive those who have been inadequate friends:**

- Those who have rejected my tentative and feeble efforts to reach out.

- Those who refuse to forgive me for things I have done that have damaged a relationship.

- Those who don't know how to be a friend unless I do all the calling, seeking out, initiating.

- Those who can never share beyond a superficial level.

- Those who know how to befriend me when I am in need, but cut off the relationship when I am functioning well.

- Those who destroy a possible relationship because they "don't want to bother me," and consequently leave no foundation on which to build.[3]

Pray blessings prayers on all those you have forgiven. If someone came to your mind, but you could not yet honestly forgive, ask God to help you want to forgive. If no one specific came to your mind, ask God to help you always have a forgiving spirit.

Thank God for His forgiveness to you.

## Scripture for This Week

(MATT. 6:14-15; MARK 11:22-26; AND LUKE 6:35-38)

Read Matt. 6:14-15: Ask God to show you anyone else you need to forgive. If you did forgive, thank God for helping you to forgive.

Meditate on Mark 11:22-26.

Practice Luke 6:35-38.

## Praying Scripture

(LUKE 6:35-38)

*Dear Jesus,*

*Only by your power can I forgive and refrain from judging, criticizing, and condemning others. Help me see people through your eyes. Give me a heart of compassion and forgiveness. Amen.*

## Song from Luke 6:35-26

Judge not, and you shall not be judged.

Don't criticize or condemn.

Forgive and you'll be forgiven.

Show compassion as your Father does.

Give and your gift will return to you

In full and overflowing measure,

Shaken together to make room for more.

Whatever measure you use, great or small

Will be used to measure what is given back to you.

# LAUGH OFTEN

Four-year-old Marissa and I were finishing a walk on a paved trail near her home when she began to run ahead of me. She looked back once to see me far behind and then continued running. I decided to sneak up on her, so I began running quickly but quietly to catch her. When she turned around and saw me running in my sneaky way, she ran faster, then plopped on the ground laughing hysterically as the ribbon fell off her ponytail and almost slid into the drain. I dropped down beside her laughing with her. She laughed even harder, and we could not stop. She reminded me of that day not long ago and that got us started laughing all over again.

Generally, children seem to laugh a lot more each day than adults do. It might be a good idea for us to take a dose of laughter medicine from children. Proverbs 17:22 tells us, "A cheerful heart is good medicine" (NLT). I like to paraphrase that verse: "Laughter does good like medicine."

"For the happy heart; life is a continual feast" (Prov. 15:15, NLT). One day after class, the professor next door to my husband's college classroom told him that the students next door could hear the laughter and wanted to come join the fun. Just last Sunday, the Sunday School class I was attending was filled with laughter. A gentleman came to collect the attendance book and said, "You're having too much fun in here." People gravitate to laughter because it cheers the heart.

Our puppet team used the "Laughter Song" during Vacation Bible School. The lyrics consist entirely of "Ha, ha, ha." The children love it so much that we decided to include it in the closing program for parents. At the first note and ha-ha, the children began squealing with delight. Even adults who were trying their hardest to keep their composure began to laugh, some hysterically. Laughter is contagious!

Proverbs 15:13 says: "A glad heart makes a happy face" (NLT). Laughter, smiles, gladness, joy, thanksgiving, and rejoicing are interconnected.

When Marissa was two, she stayed with us while her parents were moving. I taught her Phil. 4:4: "Rejoice in the Lord always; I will say it again: Rejoice!" She could recite it clearly, complete with reference, when she saw her parents the next week. I also taught her a song that goes with that scripture. A couple of weeks ago she called to interview me as part of a project she was doing for her second-grade class. She asked me to name my favorite song when I was seven—the age she is now. I told her I loved to sing and liked lots of songs but didn't have a favorite. She said, "I know your favorite song now." When I asked her what it is, she whispered in the phone: "Rejoice!" I smiled and agreed that I like that song. A singing, rejoicing heart is a glad heart.

Another children's song about joy comes from Neh. 8:10: "The joy of the LORD is your strength" (NKJV). I do not think it is sacrilegious to imagine that God smiled when He created the elephant and giraffe and perhaps laughed out loud when He created the monkey. I am sure He had a happy feeling every time He said, "It is good!" He had to be smiling:

- when He gave Eve to Adam

- when He gave Noah a rainbow

- when He gave Abraham a lamb to sacrifice in place of Isaac

Even Isaac's name means "he laughed." Dr. Dennis Kinlaw proposed in a speech on prayer that Isaac's name means "God laughed," because God knew the plan for man's redemption was now in place. Through Isaac's seed, the Messiah would and did come!

Jesus himself said: "As the Father has loved me, so have I loved you. Now remain in my love. If you obey my commands, you will remain in my love, just as I have obeyed my Father's commands and remain in his love. I have told you this so that my joy may be in you and that your joy may be complete" (John 15:9-11). Scripture shows us that Jesus spread joy and had a good time. He must have enjoyed the wedding feast at Cana of Galilee and His meal with Zacchaeus. I can see Him throwing His head back in laughter as the multitudes feasted on the loaves and fish and at the look on Peter's face when he pulled in the nets laden with fish. I think He giggled with the children when He held them on His lap and blessed them. No doubt He smiled when He saw Lazarus come forth from the grave. His heart was made glad when the widow gave her last cent to the temple treasury. Even with a heavy heart, I believe He smiled and waved at the crowd welcoming Him as He made His triumphal entry into Jerusalem. He implied in Matt. 11:16-19 that He enjoyed feasting, fellowship, and festivities.

How long has it been since you had a good laugh? If it's been awhile, put laughter back into your life. Buy a children's joke book if necessary for some good, clean laughs, and tell one of the jokes to someone else who needs a chuckle. Think of a delightful event in your past. Remember it, smile, and give thanks.

Over the past four weeks we've examined some of our painful memories. This week, let's remember times of laughter and joy. We need balance. Ecclesiastes 3:4 says: "[There is] a time to weep and a time to laugh." Lighten up. Rejoice! I will say it again: Rejoice!

## Increase Your Spiritual Awareness

- Purposefully include joy, laughter, singing, and thanksgiving in your prayers this week.
- Invite a friend to lunch and talk about joyful and laughter-filled memories. Pray a prayer of thanks and rejoicing.
- Make a long list of reasons for rejoicing:
  Examples:  Rejoice in your salvation.
  Rejoice in the forgiveness of sins.
  Rejoice in God's love.
- Smile often. Smile when no one else is around. Smile in the dark. Smile as you extend prayers of thanksgiving.

## Scripture for This Week

(PROV. 15:13, 15,30; 17:22; NEH. 8:10; JOHN 15:11, 16:24; PHIL. 4:4)

Memorize Phil. 4:4 and repeat it daily.

Day 1: Prov. 15:13: "A happy heart makes the face cheerful, but heartache crushes the spirit." Give thanks for healing God has brought to your spirit.

Day 2: Prov. 15:15: "The cheerful heart has a continual feast." Give thanks for God's provisions.

Day 3: Prov. 15:30: "A cheerful look brings joy to the heart, and good news gives health to the bones." Smile and think of God's love.

Day 4: Prov. 17:22: "A cheerful heart is good medicine, but a crushed spirit dries up the bones." Think of laughter as good medicine.

Day 5: Neh. 8:10: "For the joy of the LORD is your strength." Give thanks for joy and strength.

Day 6: John 15:11: "I have told you this so that my joy may be in you and that your joy may be complete." Ask for His joy in you.

Day 7: John 16:24: "Ask and you will receive, and your joy will be complete." Ask and receive His complete joy.

## Praying Scripture

(PHIL. 4:4-5)

*Lord,*

*Remind me often to rejoice in you. Your joy gives me strength. I want to spread cheer from the well of abundant joy you have given me and to do it with a gentle spirit. Amen.*

## Song from Philippians 4:4

Rejoice in the Lord always; I will say it again: Rejoice.
Rejoice in the Lord always; I will say it again: Rejoice.
Let your gentleness be evident to all; the Lord is near.
Let your gentleness be evident to all; the Lord is near.

# ACCEPT YOURSELF

I love photographs. I'm not good at taking them, but I love to look at them. I usually cut off the head or legs or an arm of my subject. I'm not a photographer, but I think it's great fun to get out the old picture albums to see how much I've changed and how others have changed.

My grandmother's home had a parlor that was rarely used by the family. It contained a piano, organ, shelves of books, sofa, chairs, and photos everywhere. I spent hours in that room trying to play the old pump organ and looking at the photos of my grandparents, aunts, and uncles in their younger years. Thinking of the wedding pictures and bridal portraits that were there reminds me of my own.

My bridal portrait was taken a few weeks before my wedding. According to the contract I signed, it would be taken in the photo studio and I was to be given two glossy prints to be used in the newspaper the day after my wedding.

A college friend had recently gotten married and was going to let me wear her dress. Her wedding was in another state during the

Christmas holidays, and I had not attended. I had never seen her dress—only photos. But it was beautiful on her. She and I were nearly the same size, and we were certain it would fit me.

When the time drew near to schedule my bridal portrait sitting, Marty brought the dress over and left it in my room. It was gorgeous, and I could hardly wait to try it on. Much to my dismay, it did not fit. It hung off my shoulders, the waist was too big, and the sleeves and dress itself were too long. But I felt I had no options. I didn't know anyone else close to my size who had a wedding dress available. There was no budget to purchase a wedding dress, and no time to shop for one anyway. I don't know if I thought maybe I would grow into the dress or if I convinced myself no one would notice, but I decided to wear it for the bridal portrait and scheduled the appointment.

Everyone knows you need a super hairdo for your bridal portrait, so I saved my money and made an appointment with the hair stylist. It looked just awful! Nonetheless, the next day a friend borrowed her boyfriend's car, drove me downtown, and helped me unload a carload of lace and net. She zipped, buttoned, and pinned me into the too-large wedding dress. To make matters worse, the photographer on duty was new. I felt quite sure he had never taken a bridal portrait.

When the proofs came back, I was reduced to tears. The picture didn't even look like me. The dress that looked beautiful on my friend, looked ugly on me, and it didn't fit. It wasn't *made* for me. The hairstyle wasn't mine—it was created by someone who didn't even know me.

I ended up destroying the proofs, rearranged my budget, bought a dress, and rescheduled my bridal portrait sitting. I found the dress just for me in my size—and it fit my personality. I did my own hair for the second visit to the photographer—a photographer with bridal portrait experience. The result was much more satisfactory. It looked like me.

The pictures we cherish most of friends and relatives are not the glamour shots. We prize the photos in which our loved ones look like themselves—as if they could step out of the portrait and speak to us. Yes, the best portraits are those in which we look natural. Real life is the same way. Be yourself. Accept yourself.

Irene Harrell tells a delightful story in her book *Ordinary Days with an Extraordinary God* about her family's visit to the county fair. They were viewing the livestock exhibits when a big, pink, prize pig darted across the pen. Her little daughter, Alice, squealed with delight, "That pig looks just like me!" Irene prayed this prayer: "O Lord, what joy little children have! I'd be embarrassed to think that a pig looked like me and would certainly never voice such an opinion. Make me humble enough to recognize that being an honest pig is preferable to being me when I'm trying to be what I am not."[1]

It is difficult to be free and honest and accept ourselves if we don't know our inmost hearts. Our creator, designer, has insights to reveal to us about ourselves if only we will seek and receive that truth. There is freedom in allowing God to totally expose who we are and what we can be through Him.

One of the reasons I was so unhappy with my first set of bridal portrait proofs was because of the inexperienced photographer. A well-trained photographer knows just the right angle and pose to bring out our best features. Jesus, like a master photographer or artist, knows how to bring out our best features in real life. Allow Him to help you see and accept yourself through His eyes. Give Him the brush and let Him paint your portrait. Reflect on the words of this song:

## The Brush
### Lyrics by Chuck Milhuff

Life started out like a canvas,

And God started painting on me,

But I took the paint brush from Jesus,

And painted what I wished to see;

The colors I painted kept running,

And the objects were all out of size.

I had made a mess of my painting,

My way now seemed so unwise.

So I brought my painting to Jesus,

All the colors, all the pieces, so wrong,

In the markets of earth it was worthless,

But His blood made my painting belong.

He worked with no condemnation,

Never mentioned the mess I had made,

Then He dipped His brush in the rainbow,

And signed it, "The price has been paid."

When I gave the brush back to Jesus,

When I gave the brush back to Him,

He started all over life's canvas to fill,

When I gave to Jesus the brush of my will.*

## Increase Your Spiritual Awareness

Look at some photos of yourself this week—of your childhood, your teen years, and recent photos.

*Chuck Millhuff, "The Brush," © Copyright 1975, Renewed 2003. Ben Speer Music/SESAC (admin. by ICG). Used by permission.

Ask God to reveal insight to you about your personality, gifts, masks you may have put in place, walls you have erected for self-protection, emotions you have blocked, and ways you may be deceiving yourself. Let Him guide your heart's search and free you to be yourself, to accept yourself as He paints your portrait from His eyes.

## Scripture for This Week

(PHIL. 1:3-6; PS. 119:29; AND ROM. 5:1-2)

Memorize Phil. 1:6: "Being confident of this, that he who began a good work in you will carry it on to completion until the day of Christ Jesus."

Meditate on Ps. 119:29: "Keep me from lying to myself; give me the privilege of knowing your law" (NLT).

Read Rom. 5:1-2 aloud daily: "So now, since we have been made right in God's sight by faith in his promises, we can have real peace with him because of what Jesus Christ our Lord has done for us. For because of our faith, he has brought us into this place of highest privilege where we now stand, and we confidently and joyfully look forward to actually becoming all that God has had in mind for us to be" (TLB).

## Praying Scripture

(PHIL. 1:6 AND ROM. 5:1-2)

*Dear God,*

*Master Creator, you know me better than I know myself. You have taught me many things about myself that I would not have recognized without your help. As Paul prayed for the saints at Philippi, I too have the confidence that you who began a good work in me will be faithful to carry it on to completion. Continue your workmanship in me, and with confidence and joy I look forward to becoming all you have in mind for me to be. Amen.*

## Song from Romans 5:1-2

We have been made right in God's sight
by faith in His promises.
We now have true peace in our hearts
because of what our Lord has done for us.
Because of our faith, Christ brought us to this place,
A place of highest privilege where we now stand.
With confidence and joy we look forward to becoming
All God has in mind for us to be.

# PICTURE
# YOUR PRAYERS

I don't take a lot of photos. My headless, limbless specimens have kept my family laughing for years. Even so, I have collected quite an assortment of photo albums, framed portraits, and boxes of pictures. I can't seem to let go of any pictures that come my way from students, family, or friends. I get photos in Christmas letters and as gifts. I get school pictures from nieces, nephews, and grandchildren. Practically every room in my home displays photos of children and grandchildren—including the laundry room. They just keep accumulating filling photo boxes, picture racks, albums, and frames. There are photos on the refrigerator, counter, shelves, walls, desk, piano, tables, mantle, dresser, and almost everywhere there is an empty spot. I often use pictures as inspiration for prayer. It makes my prayer time memorable and fun.

Last week I suggested you use pictures of yourself as a tool for praying for yourself. This week I will share some ways you can use pictures to make your prayer times for others meaningful.

I have a friend who assembled an album specifically for her prayer times. She included pictures, business cards, printed articles, and other reminders of people, churches, and situations on her prayer list.

A number of years ago someone gave me a prayer pocket to use during my prayer time. It looks like a large, cloth, greeting card envelope. When opened, there's a pocket in both the bottom and the flap of the envelope. I have pictures, notes, prayer lists, missionary bookmarks, information about the Jesus film, and prayer requests I've been given. It's amazing how much this prayer pocket holds!

I also have a larger folder with pockets on each side when it's open. It holds prayer reminders too big to fit into the cloth prayer pocket.

I do not take all of these to my prayer time every day because I have other sources of prayer lists and requests such as loose-leaf notebooks and spiral notebooks. These contain information on prayer team members and specific groups of people. I rotate them and allow God to lead. I have found my prayers to be more effective when I ask God to show me where my prayer focus is to be for the day and pray very specific prayers centered on those needs.

If you have never used prayer tools, begin with picturing your prayers. Of all the prayer aids I use, I find photos to be one of the most beneficial. I believe you will find it an effective way to pray for those dear to you.

## Increase Your Spiritual Awareness

Use your family photo albums as you pray this week. Turn to the first page and choose a person for focused prayer. Stay with one person until you sense God releasing you. This will keep you from flitting from page to page and feeling as if you have prayed no significant prayer for any one person. Keep your prayer journal close at hand. Write down the specific ways you have prayed for each individual. Choose a verse and pray scripture for the person for whom you are interceding. Continue using this plan in the days ahead for other family members and friends in the album. The photos will give you a visual prompt to pray in specific ways as you remember past events.

In addition to using photo albums as a prayer tool, breathe a prayer for individuals in photos displayed in your home as you move from room to room.

Examples:

Give _____ wisdom today in the decisions he must make.

Be with _____ as she begins second grade today.

Help _____ to always be a woman of truth.

Protect _____.

Touch _____ physically.

In this way you can be in nearly constant prayer for your loved ones.

## Scripture for This Week

(2 TIM. 1 AND 4, AND EPH. 1:15-23)

Read Paul's prayer in Eph. 1:15-16 and pray it for your loved ones.

As you read the first and last chapters of 2 Tim., you find the apostle Paul imprisoned in Rome and realizing that he is near the end of his life. He gives his beloved Timothy parting advice. Portions of these chapters read like a photo album as Paul reminisces about those who have been faithful and those who have abandoned him.

As you pray using your photo albums, you will find yourself smiling at some pictures and weeping at others. Turn some of Paul's wisdom into a prayer for your loved ones.

"For God did not give us a spirit of timidity, but a spirit of power, of love and of self-discipline" (2 Tim. 1:7).

"I know whom I have believed and am convinced that he is able to guard what I have entrusted to him for that day." (2 Tim. 1:12).

"Guard the good deposit that was entrusted to you—guard it with the help of the Holy Spirit who lives in us" (2 Tim. 1:14).

"But you, keep your head in all situations, endure hardship, do the work of an evangelist, discharge all the duties of your ministry" (2 Tim 4:5).

"The Lord will rescue me from every evil attack and will bring me safely to his heavenly kingdom. To him be glory for ever and ever. Amen" (2 Tim. 4:18).

"The Lord be with your spirit. Grace be with you" (2 Tim. 4:22).

## Praying Scripture

(2 TIM. 1)

*Heavenly Father,*

*When I read Paul's letter to Timothy, my heart is warmed. I sense the love he has when he calls Timothy his dear son and prays that the Father and Christ Jesus our Lord will shower Timothy with kindness, mercy, and peace. Paul reminds Timothy that he prays for him every day and many times during the long nights begs God to bless him richly. These are the prayers I want to extend to my faithful loved ones. I pray for myself and those dear to me that we who have accepted God's gift of the Holy Spirit will be wise and strong—that we will not be afraid of people but will love them and enjoy being with them. Stir this inner power within me so that I will never be afraid to tell others about my Lord! Amen.*

## Song from Ephesians 1:17-19

I pray that God,
The glorious Father of our Lord Jesus Christ
Will extend the Spirit of wisdom
So that you may see Him clearly.
And may the eyes of your heart be enlightened
So that you can see the future
He has called you to share:
The hope of the riches of His glorious inheritance,
And His incredible power to those who believe.

# SURPRISE SOMEONE WITH KINDNESS

It was Friday afternoon of a busy week teaching fourth graders when I boarded the plane with my brand-new, carry-on suitcase. I had carefully chosen just the right size to fit into the overhead bins of an airplane so I wouldn't have to check baggage. My husband and I were traveling separately to the dedication of the new sanctuary in an Ohio church. He traveled by automobile from our home in Traverse City, Michigan, to fulfill speaking engagements along the way. I sent my clothes for the weekend with Curtis and packed my new carry-on with toiletries and a few things I had forgotten to send with him. I didn't realize how heavy it was until I tried to lift it into the overhead compartment. As I slowly followed passengers down the narrow aisle of the plane, I could see that the storage space surrounding my seat was full, but I noticed an opening a couple of rows in front of my seat. As I began to lift my luggage above the heads of already-seated passengers, I realized I didn't have the strength to lift it high enough to avoid the ducking heads below. A gentleman sitting across the aisle in the row just before mine stepped up and without a word carefully lifted my bag into the overhead. With a grateful heart I thanked him as he looked straight ahead and nodded ever so slightly. It was as if he had done exactly what he was supposed to do with no acknowledgement required or expected.

I fretted the entire flight, wondering how I could retrieve my luggage without dropping it or bumping someone's head. I decided I'd wait and be the last passenger to exit. The three persons in the row in front of me had moved forward when the gentleman across the aisle stood and reached into the bin that contained my luggage. I assumed he had baggage stored there also. I was wrong. He picked up my bag, placed it in the empty aisle seat directly in front of me, and without looking back moved quickly down the aisle. I said "Thank you!" but he never acknowledged that he heard me. By the time I exited the plane, my stranger-friend was nowhere in sight. I looked for him as I moved through the airport and waited for Curtis to meet me, but I never located him to give him proper thanks.

I will probably never see this kind gentleman again or know his name, but I will forever remember that thoughtful, random act of kindness.

Has something similar happened to you? Doesn't it make you smile even today?

## Increase Your Spiritual Awareness

Wouldn't it be fun to surprise someone every day this week with an unexpected act of kindness—no strings attached? Stay prayerfully alert to the needs of others around you. At least once each day extend grace to one of God's creatures. After your courteous act, keep that individual's face forefront in your mind and breathe prayers of blessing and hope for him or her. Ask God to give you specific ways to pray for this person whom you may never meet again.

## Scripture for This Week

(COL. 3)

Read Chapter 3 each day. Memorize verse 12. Practice putting on mercy, kindness, humility, and gentleness. "Therefore, as God's chosen people, holy and dearly loved, clothe yourselves with compassion, kindness, humility, gentleness, and patience" (Col. 3:12).

## Praying Scripture

(COL. 3:12-17)

*Lord Jesus,*

*Teach me to show tenderhearted mercy and kindness to others. Forgive me for worrying about making a good impression on them. I want to be a person who is gentle and forgiving, letting love guide my life. Your words enrich my life. I want my words and deeds to enrich the lives of others. I acknowledge that the peace I have in my heart comes from you. Thank you. Amen.*

### Song from Colossians 3:15-17

Let the peace of God which comes from Christ
Always be present in your hearts and lives.
Let the words of Christ enrich your lives.
As you teach them to each other,
Sing them unto the Lord.
Whatever you do or say, let it represent the Lord.
Come with Him into God's presence
To give Him your thanks.

# LEAD
# BY EXAMPLE

It was snowing in Nashville and, according to the weather reports, across the nation. I was scheduled to return home to Traverse City, Michigan, on Sunday, January 2, after visiting my brother and extended family over New Year's. After church, I called the airport to make sure my flight from Nashville was not cancelled as well as my connecting flight from Chicago to Traverse City. I was told that all was well. I was relieved because my teaching duties were scheduled to resume on the 3rd.

When I arrived in Chicago, I learned that my flight to Traverse City had been cancelled after all—not the flight before or the one after—just mine. I was informed, along with the passengers ahead of me, that we were welcome to wait several hours for the next flight on stand-by status. The two families ahead of me demonstrated totally different reactions to the frustrating news.

The older couple immediately in front of me became surly and were rude to the attendant. They made loud demands she could not meet. The couple in front of them, although they had a tiny baby, responded with patience and courtesy. We all waited together. The young couple smiled, fed and played with the baby, and talked happily as the hours passed. The other couple continued to frown and fidget. We waited with anticipation as the names were called for stand-by passengers. Just when I thought the young couple was going to make it, a group of ticketed passengers for that flight came running to board.

It was nearly midnight as we all tried to make hotel and transportation arrangements for the remainder of the night in hopes of getting a flight out the next day.

After only a few hours of sleep, I returned to the airport early Monday morning. My new friends were already there with their baby and their smiles. I thought of them as friends although I had not spoken to them—only observed them from afar.

I have never seen that little family before or since, but, unknown to them, they eternally impacted my life. I think of them often, especially when I receive distressing airline news. They influenced my life then; they continue to influence me today.

We are all leaders, whether we want to be or not. Many times we are leading and influencing when we don't even realize that others are taking notice.

- Young children are watching parents, teachers, older children, teens.
- Teens are watching coaches, peers, sports and music idols, college students.
- College students are watching friends, professors, coworkers.
- New Christians are watching church members.

Every action has a positive or negative influence on all who watch.

## Increase Your Spiritual Awareness

Review your day yesterday. What were some of your actions that may have been observed by another person?

Example:

- Your response when the store clerk overcharged you or gave you back too much change
- Your punctuality for appointments
- Your kind words of greeting or giving the silent treatment
- Your reaction when your coworker interrupted your work or made suggestions for your project

Today is a new day. Do you owe some apologies for yesterday's behavior? Ask God to reveal insight to you in this regard. Resolve today to make those apologies if possible by phone, e-mail, card, or face-to-face.

Ask God to make you more aware tomorrow of your choices and responses, your attitudes and body language.

Tomorrow choose a block of time to be on extra alert to your attitudes and responses toward others. Example: From the time you get off work until bedtime.

As the week progresses, expand your awareness time to a half day, then a full day.

The remainder of the week, consciously continue with your awareness efforts.

Say often, "God, please make me more aware of my actions. Show me how to lead like Jesus."

If you follow the plan, you will become more aware that every action has a positive or negative influence on another individual.

(2 COR. 3)

Look in the mirror each day and remind yourself that you can be a person who reflects the glory of the Lord as His Spirit works within you to make you more and more like Christ.

(2 COR. 3:17-18)

*Lord,*

*My heart is grateful that you have given me life. Thank you for the freedom you have given me through the forgiveness of sins. I want to be a reflection of your glory. Holy Spirit, I give you permission to work within me to make me more and more like Christ. Amen.*

## Song from 2 Corinthians 3:17-18

The Lord is the Spirit who gives life.
In Him there is freedom from sin.
We as Christians have no veil on our faces.
We can brightly reflect the glory of the Lord.
As the Spirit of the Lord works within us
We become more and more like Him.

# IMPACT
# YOUR WORLD

I didn't realize the impact one praying woman could have on her world until I met Gertrude Taylor. I was invited to her home to attend a prayer group she led made up of seminary wives. She had agreed to meet periodically with the seminary wives in her home but would not allow the gathering to be announced publicly. She wanted it to be a group that God put together that would meet quietly and sincerely to seek His guidance.

Gertrude prayed about everything, and she gave us prayer assignments. I remember her suggestion that we breathe a prayer for strangers we met along the streets. She challenged us that every prayer has significance, and we never know how far-reaching our prayers are. She asked us to look into the eyes of an individual and say a silent prayer for him or her. I began to really see people as people rather than just blurs I passed as I shopped, walked, and ran errands.

Taking a praise walk through her home was one of the first things Mrs. Taylor did every morning. She lifted her hands and spoke words of praise as she worshipped God in the early moments of her day.

She also prayed for a hedge of protection around wayward children, and that made a deep impression on me. My husband and I were senior high ministries directors of our church, and I remember her calling some of those teens by name as she prayed for God to build a wall of protection around them until they came to Him.

Gertrude Taylor was a gracious lady. She had a word of encouragement for all. We attended the same church, and she sat just behind the rows of teens on the front-left side of the sanctuary where we usually sat. I often overheard her speaking complimentary and endearing words to teens and adults alike. It was evident that she really cared.

We were in our first church assignment following seminary when my husband asked me to start a ladies' prayer group. I used many of the ideas Gertrude Taylor modeled for me. The word spread around our church that if you wanted a prayer answered, give your request to the ladies' prayer group. After witnessing the amazing answers to prayer, the men began their own prayer meetings at the church a couple of times a week. Our church was in a perpetual revival during those days, and we saw miracles, salvations, healings, growth. A few years ago I received a phone call from a lady who had been a young teen in our church during that time. She was beginning a ladies' group in her church, and her mother suggested she call me for some of the ideas I used when her mother was in our women's prayer fellowship. The dividends of prayer investment are astounding. We never know who is watching and following in our footsteps.

Gertrude Taylor is in heaven now. I am glad I took opportunities when she was living to tell her how greatly she touched my life. Who are some individuals who have impacted your Christian walk? Today would be a perfect time to reflect on their teachings and let them know how much you appreciate their influence in your life.

## Increase Your Spiritual Awareness

Make a list of some of the people who have had a positive spiritual influence on your life. Give thanks for each person you can remember who God used to bring you into a closer relationship with Him: family, friends, teachers, pastors, authors, musicians, artists, counselors, coworkers, etc.

If those individuals are alive, pray for them.

Consider writing a note of appreciation or making a phone call to some of these individuals.

Pray that your own life will be a godly example to everyone you meet.

Ask someone close to you how you are doing at home, at work, at church.

Apply some of Gertrude Taylor's prayer ideas:

- Pray for those you meet on the street. Ask God to help you see them through His eyes.
- Take a praise walk early in the morning.
- Pray a hedge of protection around wayward children.
- Give words of encouragement to others this week.

## Scripture for This Week

(1 TIM. 4:7-16)

Meditate on these thoughts:

- Spend your time and energy in the exercise of keeping spiritually fit (v. 7).

- Our hope is in the living God who died for all (v. 10).

- Do not let anyone think little of you because you are young. Be their ideal; let them follow the way you teach and live; be a pattern for them in your love, your faith, and your clean thoughts (vs. 11-12).

- Be sure to use the abilities God has given you (vs. 14-15).

- Keep a close watch on all you do and think (v. 16).

- Stay true to what is right, and God will bless you and use you to help others (v. 16b).

## Praying Scripture

(1 TIM. 4:7-16)

*Dear God,*

*I want to spend my time and energy where it counts and be spiritually fit for any task you place before me. I am aware that my life is influencing others even when I am unaware that others are watching. It is my desire to teach truth and be a pattern in your love to others. I yearn to have a strong faith and clean thoughts. I will use the abilities you have given me and throw myself wholeheartedly into your work as I keep a close watch on all I think and do. My hope is in you, the Living God, my salvation. Amen.*

## Song from 1 Timothy 4

My hope is in the Living God who died for all.
I have accepted His salvation.
I will be a pattern
In love, in faith, in purity.
I will closely watch all I think and do.
My hope is in the Living God who died for me.
I have accepted His salvation.
I'll stay true to right and good;
I will use my talents for the Lord.
And God will bless and use me to help others.

# EXTEND
# LOVE

My three-year-old grandson, Calvin, called me on Mother's Day. He said, "Happy Mother's Day, Mimi," and began singing, "Happy birthday." Calvin believes every celebration day that includes a cake or a greeting that begins with the word happy calls for the "Happy Birthday" song.

After we talked for a while, I asked him, "Did you give your mom a hug and wish her happy Mother's Day today?"

He responded in a very sad voice, "No, but I wish I did."

I explained to him, "It's still Mother's Day, and you can do it when you get off the phone."

He ended the phone conversation abruptly and told me goodbye. As he handed the telephone to his mother, there was a delay before she spoke. I could hear her conversation with Calvin and knew what was happening. When she finally began to speak to me, there was laughter in her voice. She said, "Sorry for the delay; Calvin just wanted to give me a big hug and wish me happy Mother's Day. Isn't that sweet?"

Have there been times when you felt like Calvin and wished you had given someone a hug or a word of encouragement but missed the opportunity? As long as your loved ones are alive and it is still called today, you can, as Calvin did, take advantage of the moment.

Hebrews 3:13 says: "But encourage one another daily, as long as it is called Today, so that none of you may be hardened by sin's deceitfulness."

## Increase Your Spiritual Awareness

Extend God's love to someone in a tangible way each day this week. Give hugs, speak words of praise, smile, wave. Freely hand out compliments. Encourage. Pray.

## Scripture for This Week

(HEB. 3)

Read portions of Heb. 3 each day. Practice Heb. 3:13. Try to memorize it, and repeat it often.

## Praying Scripture

(HEB. 3:12-15)

*Jesus,*

*Soften my heart. I do not want to harden my heart toward anyone. When I hear the Holy Spirit speaking to me, I want to obey with a willing heart. Whom do I need to encourage today? If you lead me to someone who has been rude to me or who smells bad or who is unkempt, please help me to see that person through your eyes and to not harden my heart. I want to be faithful to the end! Amen.*

## Song from Hebrews 3:15

Harden not your heart!
Listen to my voice.
I will instruct and guide your way.
I will fill your thoughts and mind today;
I will guide and teach you what to say
If you listen to my voice and obey.

# BE PRESENT WHERE YOU ARE

Last Sunday my husband and I were traveling to a church in the country he had been to only once and I had never attended. The first two-thirds of the trip were roads we traveled frequently. We knew we were going to have to be alert when we got to the last third of the journey. We called the pastor to make sure our directions were clear, and, with our minds set at ease, we began a conversation.

Curtis was asking me questions about how this book was progressing, and I was sharing my ideas with him. At some point he interrupted me and said, "Did we pass our exit?" I replied that I didn't think so. We began watching for landmarks. Before long we saw the large green road sign saying, "Glendale—1 mile." That sign confirmed we had passed our exit. We had been so engrossed in our conversation that we were oblivious that we had missed our turn and were headed in the wrong direction.

We were reminded of the time Curtis and a friend were returning home to Nashville from the National Clergy Conference in Atlanta. They were absorbed in conversation and didn't realize they were headed toward the wrong state until they spotted a sign indicating they were near the South Carolina border—not Tennessee.

Sometimes we are so engrossed in our own world, our own purposes, our own ways, and what is happening next, that we miss what is happening now. We may be reading a book to our child or grandchild, all the while thinking about the chores waiting for us— the laundry, ironing, cooking, washing the car, running errands. Or we sit in church and our minds wander to all sorts of things. When this happens, we lose the present.

Likewise, it is possible to coast along in our Christian walk and lose sight of God's best for our day. Danger lurks when we are not spiritually alert. It is possible to slowly drift away from the source of our joy and holiness and lose our way.

I read a meaningful story many years ago about a girl who was trying to explain to her younger brother the meaning of past, present, and future. She said that the past is what happened yesterday; the future is what is happening tomorrow; and the present is what is happening today. Her next insightful words to him were, "You see, today is a gift. That is why it is called the present."

Be present where you are. This takes a little effort, concentration, and discipline, but it pays eternal dividends. Live each day to the fullest and avoid the danger of losing your way. The present is a gift!

## Increase Your Spiritual Awareness

- Look into the eyes of the person who is talking to you. Gather insights for praying for this person. Be present where you are.

- Slow down at mealtime. Smell your food. Savor the taste. Give thanks as you eat. Be present where you are.

- Be alert to the sights and sounds around you. Look for small wonders of nature. Examine the delicate intricacies of a leaf. Feel the texture. Open your senses to God's world and view things you may have missed yesterday. Pause and thank God for the everyday miracles of His creation surrounding you. Experience His nearness. Continually express gratitude to God for the beauty of nature. Be present where you are.

- Give God your full attention during your devotional times. Eliminate haste. Be present where you are.

## Scripture for This Week

(1 THESS. 4 AND 5)

Memorize 1 Thess. 5:16-18
"Be joyful always; pray continually; give thanks in all circumstances, for this is God's will for you in Christ Jesus."

## Praying Scripture

(1 THESS. 5:11-23)

*Dear God,*

*I do not know the day of your returning, but I want to live every day to the fullest, always watchful, alert, and ready for your return. While I wait, I want to please you in my daily living, to encourage others and build them up, to be joyful, and to keep praying with thanksgiving no matter what happens. I know this is your will. I want you to make me entirely pure and devoted to you. Keep my spirit, soul, and body strong and blameless until that day when the Lord Jesus Christ comes back again. Amen.*

## Song from 1 Thessalonians 5:16-18

Always be joyful;
Keep on praying;
No matter what happens, give thanks,
For this is God's will for those in Christ Jesus,
Be joyful. Keep praying. Give thanks!
Be joyful. Keep praying. Give thanks!

# PRACTICE HIS PRESENCE

Our two-year-old granddaughter was talking to her grandpa and me on the phone and telling us that she was making things with play-dough. Suddenly she said, "Let me show you something." At that point the phone went silent. We kept talking to her, but she wasn't responding. Finally, her mother, who had not heard Kiersten's comment, came to the phone, and said, "I don't know what happened. Kiersten just stood the phone up on the counter and started playing at her play-dough table." Curtis and I both chuckled; we knew exactly what had happened. We could envision it because we knew that the play-dough table was in the kitchen near the counter. She had positioned the phone where she thought we could see her making her creations.

A few months ago I experienced a similar situation with our three-year-old grandson when he said over the phone, "Mimi, watch me." His mother came to the phone laughing. She said he set the phone on the living room sofa and proceeded to do his antics in the middle of the floor, quite sure I could see him perform.

Because they could hear our voices on the telephone, we seemed so close, so real, they were just sure we could see what they were doing.

Aren't there times when God seems so close to you and His presence is so real that you feel He can surely see you obey Him? There are times we want Him to watch and tell us we are doing things right, or we want His advice and guidance. Maybe we just want Him to watch us work for companionship so we don't feel so alone.

There are other times in life when He seems far away. Times may be difficult. We have called on Him for help, but nothing seems to be happening. We can't hear His voice, yet we desperately want to know that He is there.

Occasionally He pays us a surprise visit. He comes unexpectedly at an unusual time or in a surprising way.

Hagar experienced this in the wilderness when she was running away from her mistress, Sarai, who had mistreated her. You can read this story in Gen. 16:7-10.

> The angel of the LORD found Hagar near a spring in the desert; it was the spring that is beside the road to Shur. And he said, "Hagar, servant of Sarai, where have you come from, and where are you going?"
>
> "I'm running away from my mistress Sarai," she answered.
>
> Then the angel of the LORD told her, "Go back to your mistress and submit to her." The angel added, "I will so increase your descendants that they will be too numerous to count."

In verses 11 and 12, the angel of the Lord spoke more to Hagar about the child she was carrying, then Hagar gave God a name.

> She gave this name to the LORD who spoke to her: "You are the God who sees me," for she said, "I have now seen the One who sees me" (Gen. 4:13).

The *New Revised Standard* says she named Him El-roi. I like that—El-roi, the God who sees!

Be assured that He sees. Whatever your situation, He is watching.

Last week we practiced being present where we are and increased our awareness of our surroundings and task at hand. This week we are going to heighten our awareness of God's presence.

## Increase Your Spiritual Awareness

Repeat these words often: "Thank you, God, for your presence. You are here. You are El-roi, the God who sees me."

Say it when you get out of bed. Speak it aloud in the car on the way to work or school. Whisper it throughout the day. Repeat it in your thoughts. Add it to your mealtime blessings. Recite it again at bedtime.

## Scripture for This Week

(GEN. 16 AND ZEPH. 3:17)

Read the story of Hagar in Genesis, chapter 16.

Read Zeph. 3:17. "The LORD your God is with you, he is mighty to save. He will take great delight in you, he will quiet you with his love, he will rejoice over you with singing." Meditate on this passage. Visualize God saying to you that He is with you and will rejoice over you with singing. How does this make you feel? Carry that thought with you throughout the week.

(ZEPH. 3:17)

*My Loving Heavenly Father,*

*It amazes me that you, who are mighty to save, take delight in me! It is even more amazing to visualize you rejoicing over me with singing, yet it brings me inexpressible gladness! Your love quiets my heart and gives me peace. Thank you, dear God, that you are with me right now; you are El-roi, the God who sees me! Amen.*

### Song from Zephaniah 3:17

I, the Lord your God, am with you.
Mighty to save, I take delight in you.
I will quiet you with My love
And rejoice o're you with singing.
I, the Lord your God, am with you.

# READ
# A BOOK

It startled me when well-known speaker Florence Littauer said that the average person does not read a book a year and many individuals do not complete an entire book in his or her lifetime.

I am a reader! The summer I was seven, we moved to a town several hours away from cousins and friends. My father had been hired as principal of the elementary school where I would be entering third grade. As we toured the school, my sister, five years older than I, located the library and asked Daddy if she could take home a book to read. I followed her example and chose a book or two for myself. As the summer progressed, my sister introduced me to biographies. Nothing about the plain orange hardback covers enticed me to read those books, but my sister could not put them down. She brought home stacks at a time and read all of them in a few days. I was intrigued and began reading them myself. Before the summer was over and the fall semester began, I read several biographies and continued reading them until I had read all the books in the series that the library owned.

We lived across the road from the public library during my eighth grade of school. It was a small village, and the library was not open every day. I brought home as many books as I could carry, or at least as many as the librarian allowed. I devoured those teen fictions, sometimes reading a book a day in the summer.

As an adult I have found myself more enticed by self-help and personal development books that share elements of real-life stories. I have discovered that many of these books are biographies with a purpose and are more exciting than fiction.

Currently I am reading several books. I start one and before I can finish, I am intrigued by a new title; or someone gives me a book he or she highly recommends, and before I know it I'm into the introduction and chapter one. Among the books I am reading now are:

- *The Heavenly Man,* a book I can read only in small doses because of the pain and persecution he has suffered for his Christian faith

- *Dream Big,* a book about Henrietta Mears recommended by Becky Tirabassi in the book *The Burning Heart Contract* that I recently finished

- *Lord, I Want to Be Whole* by Stormie Omartian, a book that I have read many times and given to more than a hundred individuals and church libraries

- Dennis Kinlaw's *This Day with the Master* that my husband and I are both reading as a devotional guide

- *The Torn Veil* that I finished reading in just a couple of days (I couldn't put down this Muslim lady's story of her conversion to Christianity.)

- A book just published by a friend entitled *The Bare Bones of Healing* that is an interactive study on resurrecting life from a painful past based on my friend's journey to restoration (As a foundation she uses the story from Ezek. 37 of dry bones living again.)

I won't mention the titles of a couple of unfinished books I cannot quite get into. However, since I am a closure person, I will finish them eventually. With that testimonial, I want to release *you* from reading a book that is boring to you. I have often told my students to discard an uninteresting book and find one more inviting. Why waste valuable time reading reluctantly when there are a host of exciting books waiting to be read?

My husband and children share my love for reading. My husband packed nearly a hundred boxes of books during our last move, and that was after giving stacks of books away. We have books everywhere in our home—in baskets beside chairs, on the bedside tables, on the footstool, on the bookshelves in the hall, foyer, kitchen, bedrooms, family room, and both offices. Curtis is very territorial about his books. He doesn't like for me to read them before he is finished. He says I am tempted to read quotes to him and tell him about the book when he wants to read it for himself first. I get so curious about books I find lying around the house that I am often tempted to sneak and read portions.

When Mark Buchanan's first book was released, Curtis bought it right away. We were on spring break visiting our daughter. One day when he was away, I spied the book on the chest and was drawn to the title, *Your God Is Too Safe*. By the time I had read the cover and introduction, I was hooked. Since Curtis had just purchased the book and had his pen at his reading place, I knew he had not finished it yet. Still, I read on; I couldn't resist. When I heard Curtis's car pull up, I carefully placed his pen back in the book at the page where I found it and replaced the book to the top of the chest. Each time he left for a walk or to run an errand, I hurriedly picked up the book and continued reading. I started sitting in my daughter's office at the front of the house where there was a large window facing the street so I could easily see when he returned. He would slowly pass the window and pull into the driveway at the other side of the house, giving me just enough time to run to the back guest bedroom and return his book. Did I feel guilty? The book was too exciting! Eventually I confessed. That experience led me to watch for future books by Mark Buchanan.

Do you have an author like that? You read one book, and it tantalizes you to read more of that person's writing.

Maybe you aren't interested in reading and can't relate to this at all. It is possible that all you can manage to read are two or three pages of this book each week and then only because a friend or family member gave the book to you, and he or she asks you about it from time to time.

Sometimes I hear people make the comment, "I hate to read!" Or the question is asked: "Who has time to read?" I have a response. When you are reading books that give you hope and help, reading becomes meaningful and not a chore. You don't have to read massive numbers of pages to successfully complete a book. If you only read seven pages a day, you could finish a 200-page book in a month. Spend 5 to 10 minutes a day reading before bedtime, and even if you are a slow reader, you will complete a book before the end of the year and thus become, as Florence Littauer says, above average.

## Increase Your Spiritual Awareness

Read a book of the Bible. The Book of Esther is an adventurous story with only 10 chapters. Ask God what assignment He has for you "at such a time as this." I can assure you that it will be unlike Esther's task; however, each of us has a purpose to fulfill. No two stories will be identical.

Go to your church library or a Christian bookstore and prayerfully choose a book to read. Set a goal of finishing the book in one month. Decide how many minutes or pages a day you need to read to achieve your goal. You are more likely to accomplish a goal if you break it down into manageable parts. When you finish the book, you can say to yourself that you are above average!

## Scripture for This Week

### (ESTHER 1-10 AND 2 COR. 3:3)

Read a chapter or two from the Book of Esther each day, unless you just cannot put it down and have to read the entire book in one sitting. In that case, read the book twice.

Read 2 Cor. 3:3 with this thought in mind: Each of us has a biography, even if no book has been published about our life. Like Queen Esther, we have a story. God is still writing chapters, and the volume is not finished. Paul told the Corinthians that they were a letter from Christ. When people read the story or letter of your life, how are they impacted?

"Clearly, you are a letter from Christ prepared by us. It is written not with pen and ink, but with the Spirit of the living God. It is carved not on stone, but on human hearts" (NLT).

*Dear God,*

*I cannot imagine how afraid I would have been to go before the king as Queen Esther did. I hope I would have had the wisdom to call everyone I knew to fast for me as I also fasted, prayed, and prepared. I think of Mordecai's words to Esther when he said, "Who knows? Maybe you were made queen for just such a time as this." I sometimes wonder if you are saying to me in certain circumstances, I have sent you here for such a time as this. Esther's obedience challenges me: "I will go to the king even though it is forbidden. If I die; I die." Thank you for books in the Bible such as Esther's story of obedience. They bolster my faith. Thank you also for contemporary books. Many have given me hope and courage in the face of life's struggles. Yes, you still are a God of miracles! Amen.*

## Song from 2 Corinthians 3:3

You are a letter from Christ
Written not with pen and ink.
You are a letter from the Spirit of the Living God,
Not carved on stone but on the human heart.
You are a letter from Christ.

# ARM YOURSELF FOR BATTLE

One morning a family in our church decided to pray the armor prayer from Eph. 6 before leaving the house for the day. They put actions to their prayer for the benefit of their preschool daughter. First, they put on the belt of truth followed by the breastplate of righteousness. Next, they put on shoes preparing themselves to present the gospel of peace. They picked up the shield of faith, donned the helmet of salvation, and held high the sword of the Spirit. When they were finished, their four-year-old daughter asked, "Where are our pants? We need some pants!" In response, they proceeded to go through the motions of putting on Christian pants.

Through the years I lost track of this family, but when they came to my mind a couple of years ago, I decided to try to locate them. I called Information in the city where I had last known them to be living, and there was only one listing for their unusual last name. I called the number, and the daughter, now a teenager, answered the phone. After identifying myself and getting an update on her and her parents, I asked her if she remembered the armor prayer. She said, "Oh, yes! We still pray that prayer every day including putting on our Christian pants!"

Is it any wonder this family is still faithfully serving God?

I cannot say that I pray that prayer every day, but I pray it often for myself and for others. The scripture clearly states that we are in a battle, and we are not wrestling with flesh and blood but the powers of darkness and spiritual wickedness. We have been advised to take up the whole armor of God that we may be able to withstand this evil day.

## Increase Your Spiritual Awareness

Pray Eph. 6:14-18 each morning this week before you start your day. Equip yourself for whatever battle the enemy cunningly brings your way.

Concentrate on a different piece of the armor each day. Ask God to give you insight concerning each aspect of the armor. The following questions came from a spiritual warfare seminar I attended led by Dr. Chuck Lawless:

Day 1: The belt of truth. Am I the same person when no one is looking that I am in public?

Day 2: The breastplate of righteousness. Do I consistently choose to do what is right?

Day 3: Feet shod with readiness. Do I stand firmly in my faith and share Christ at all opportunities?

Day 4: The shield of faith. Do I trust God enough to do whatever He asks?

Day 5: The helmet of salvation. Is God honored by what goes on in my mind?

Day 6: The sword of the spirit. Do I study God's Word daily?

Day 7: Pray at all times. Do I live in a spirit of prayer?

## Scripture for This Week

(EPH. 6:10-18)

Study this scripture carefully each day. If possible, read it in several translations.

After reading the entire scripture passage, meditate on one verse each day.

| | |
|---|---|
| Day 1 | Verse 14 |
| Day 2 | Verse 14 |
| Day 3 | Verse 15 |
| Day 4 | Verse 16 |
| Day 5 | Verse 17 |
| Day 6 | Verse 17 |
| Day 7 | Verse 18 |

## Scripture for This Week

(EPH. 6:10-18)

*Mighty God,*

*I want to be strong in the Lord and in the power of your might. I am putting on the armor of God this morning so that I will be able to stand against the strategies of the devil. I realize that I am not wrestling against flesh and blood but against the rulers of darkness and wicked spirits. Give me discernment and watchfulness to detect the evil forces battling against me.*

*As I fasten the belt of truth, I look to my Savior for strength to reject the enemy's lies. I want to be a truthful person, not only to speak truth, but to live truth, to know truth, and to believe truth.*

*Thank you for the breastplate of righteousness. I realize that my righteousness comes from you, and Satan must flee from your righteousness. May I choose to do what is right today.*

*You have provided me with sandals of peace. Thank you for the peace that is mine. I want to share this good news of peace with those your Spirit brings into my life today.*

*I lift the shield of faith against the darts of the wicked one. Shield me from above, beneath, beside, before, and behind. Encircle me with your protection. I want to have the faith to trust you and do what you ask.*

*It is with gratitude that I put on the helmet of salvation. I recognize that my salvation comes from Jesus Christ alone. I cover my head, my mind, my thoughts, with your salvation. I want you to be honored by what I allow to come into my mind. May I have the mind of Christ.*

*The Word of God is my sword. I take this sword of the Spirit as a weapon to defeat the enemy. Help me meditate on it and memorize it so that I am ready at all times to use it to resist Satan and send him on retreat.*

*Thank you for the privilege of prayer. Show me how to intercede for others. May all my requests be in line with your Holy Spirit. I want to live in a spirit of prayer.*

*Again, I acknowledge that my strength comes from you. Amen.*

## Song from Ephesians 6:10-18

Be strong in the Lord's mighty armor;
Put on the sturdy belt of truth,
The breastplate of God's righteousness,

The shoes of peace from the good news
That you will be fully prepared.
In every battle you will need to stand firm.
Take up the shield of faith in my name.
The helmet of salvation,
The sword of the Spirit, the Word of God
That you will be fully prepared.
Pray all the time, on each occasion
In the power of the blessed Holy Spirit.
Stay alert, and don't give up
For Christians everywhere
That they will be fully prepared.

# DISCOVER TREASURES IN SURPRISING PLACES

Have you ever found an unexpected treasure in an unexpected place? I did one night when a friend invited me to go with her to an estate sale. It was my first, but she seemed right at home in this environment of clutter and people. It didn't take me long to realize that not much interested me, and I found my way to a book shelf and aimlessly leafed through books as my friend finished browsing. To my amazement, I discovered a quaint little hard-cover book with an exquisite clasp. At first I thought it might be a diary, but the gold edging and cover design led me to believe it was an ancient Bible. The title page confirmed that I had found a Holy Bible printed in 1856 by the American Bible Society. If I recall correctly, the price was only 50 cents. I went home with a treasure!

Sometimes treasures come to us in the most unexpected ways. Maybe someone has surprised you with kind words you treasure. Maybe you've made a new friend in an unexpected way. Has God sometimes answered prayer in a surprising way?

Jesus had something to say about treasures. "Do not lay up for yourselves treasures on earth, where moth and rust destroy and where thieves break in and steal; but lay up for yourselves treasures in heaven, where neither moth nor rust destroys and where thieves do not break in and steal. For where your treasure is, there your heart will be also" (Matt. 6:19-21, NKJV).

Jesus likened the Kingdom of Heaven to a treasure:

"Again, the kingdom of heaven is like treasure hidden in a field, which a man found and hid; and for joy over it he goes and sells all that he has and buys that field" (Matt. 13:44, NKJV).

Treasures are not always tangible. The Spirit of Jesus in the heart is a treasure. "But we have this treasure in earthen vessels, that the excellence of the power may be of God and not of us" (2 Cor. 4:7, NKJV).

According to Col. 2:2-3, wisdom and knowledge are treasures. In Christ "are hidden all the treasures of wisdom and knowledge" (NKJV).

Laughter, love, and acts of kindness are treasures. During Week 19 you were challenged to laugh often, in Week 25 to extend love, in Week 22 to surprise someone with kindness. Good deeds are treasures. Jesus said that when we do good deeds, we should do them secretly, and the Father in heaven will reward us (Matt. 6:1-3, NKJV). Give someone a treasure this week and look for treasures all around you.

It is possible there is a hidden treasure somewhere in your life right now even though you may be in dark circumstances. During one of the bleakest periods of my life, God revealed treasures in the darkness, secret riches that I will cherish for a lifetime. This week ask God to reveal the secret riches hidden from your view no matter what you are facing.

In Isa. 45:3, the Lord said to Cyrus: "I will give you the treasures of darkness, riches stored in secret places, so that you may know that I am the LORD, the God of Israel, who summons you by name."

Is it possible these are words the Lord wants to speak to you today?

## Increase Your Spiritual Awareness

Identify a treasure you have found in an unexpected place and give thanks. Your treasures may be gifts, words, friends, scripture, or answers to prayer.

Ask God to show you treasures that are presently lurking in your life and circumstances, treasures you have yet to recognize.

Be on the lookout each day for hidden treasures.

Sort through a trunk in the attic, a box in the garage, a junk drawer, the back corner of a closet, or a shoebox under the bed. You know the kind of place I mean. A place where you stick things you're not ready to part with. As you look through these treasures, use them to spark prayer for the people and events they bring to mind.

Be a giver of treasures.

## Scripture for This Week

(ISA. 45)

Read the entire chapter in one sitting.

Underline in your Bible or record in your journal all the references similar to verse 5: "I am the LORD, and there is no other; apart from me there is no God."

Read verse 3 each day.

Personalize portions of the chapter as if God is speaking it directly to you.

Example from Isa. 45:1-7:

"This is what I, the Lord, say to you, _____, my anointed one whose right hand I will empower. This is what the Lord says, 'I will go before you, _____. I will give you treasures hidden in the darkness—secret riches. I will do this so that you may know that I am the Lord, the God of your personal ministries who calls you by name. And why have I called you to this work? It is for the sake of Jesus Christ, my beloved son. I called you by name when you didn't even know me. I am the Lord; there is no other God."

## Praying Scripture

(ISA. 45:1-7)

*Dear God,*

*I gladly proclaim that you are the only true and living God. I am humbled and honored that you have called me to ministries ordained by you and that you have anointed me and empowered me to work alongside you. Thank you that you go before me and that you give treasures in the darkest of circumstances. You have unfolded your secret riches to me in many surprising ways. You have called me by name. With grateful heart I declare that I am yours. You are the Lord; there is no other God! Amen.*

## Song from Matthew 6:1-6

When you do a kindness, do it secretly;
Don't try to do your good deeds publicly.
Your Father in heaven who knows all secrets
Will reward you for all you do.
When you pray to me, do it secretly.
Go away and shut the door behind you.
Your Father in heaven who knows all secrets
Will reward you when you pray.
When you fast, declining foods, put on festive clothes,
Don't do it publicly as hypocrites.
Your Father in heaven who knows all secrets
Will reward you, you can be sure.
Don't store up treasures here on earth
Where they erode and thieves may steal;
Store them in heaven where they are safe;
Your heart will be there too.

# ELIMINATE COMPLAINING

I had been asked to give devotionals on the bus for a teen choir trip from Dayton, Ohio, to Anaheim, California. The choir gave concerts along the way, and the first devotional was given in the church foyer just before boarding the bus after the Sunday morning service. We were on a tight schedule since we were to give a concert in a park in Indiana that evening. I wanted to give a short devotional that would challenge the teens and sponsors before departure.

I started my challenge by stating that, although there are many things in the Bible that are difficult to understand, some verses are crystal clear. There is one verse that is very easy to understand and remember. You can memorize it easily. "Do everything without complaining or arguing" (Phil. 2:14).

No matter which version of the Bible you use, Phil. 2:14 is clear.

One translation uses the word *grumbling* instead of complaining. Is there anyone who doesn't know what complaining and grumbling mean? Another version uses the word *murmuring*. For teens, some examples might be:

- Complaining about your parents' rules.
- Grumbling about what your mom fixed for dinner.
- Murmuring about a test your teacher gave.

Other translations may use the words *quarreling* or *disputing* instead of arguing.

I grumbled a lot as a teen. Even when I didn't grumble out loud, I had a complaining spirit. I remember when a teacher overheard me murmuring about her. I was embarrassed, but it made me aware of my complaining nature. I was with a friend who wasn't a Christian, yet she never grumbled or complained. I began to think about my witness to her and others. I realize now that grumbling teens grow into complaining adults if the pattern isn't broken.

Complaining is grumbling without taking action to correct the situation or murmuring about something that cannot be fixed. Complaining is not to be confused with stating a problem to involved persons and then formulating a plan of action to resolve it.

Let's use the example of a leaky pipe under the sink.

Complaining: Every time you look under the sink you grumble about the mess to anyone who will listen.

Not Complaining: You look under the sink to determine if you can repair the pipe. If you see that neither you nor your spouse can handle it, you call in a plumber or friend or relative who can. In other words, instead of complaining, you take steps to correct the problem.

Through the years, I have used Phil. 2:14 as a model for appropriate behavior in many settings.

Complaining is often just a bad habit, but it affects others. To break a habit, one must first be aware of the problem.

Recently I have focused on the verses that follow: "So that you may become blameless and pure, children of God without fault in a crooked and depraved generation, in which you shine like stars in the universe as you hold out the word of life—in order that I may boast on the day of Christ that I did not run or labor for nothing" (Phil. 2:15-16). Now that is a passage to digest!

Verses 6-11 tell us clearly what our attitude should be, and verses 15-16 explain why. Meditate on Phil. 2:1-18 this week; it can change your life.

## Increase Your Spiritual Awareness

You guessed it! This week's challenge is to do everything without complaining and arguing. My experience has been that this is nearly impossible without prayer.

First, pray that God will alert you when you are grumbling. Ask God to make you aware each time your spirit is discontent or complaining. Chase away that attitude by speaking words of gratitude. If you realize you have affected others with your complaining attitude, apologize. But remember, even though you apologize, you may not be able to remove the negative effects of words you have already spoken. Ask God to guard your tongue before you speak and help you realize that you do not have to voice every opinion. If you recognize this as a recurring problem for you, ask God to help you have a change of heart.

Ask someone at home and someone at work to give you a "thumbs-down" signal when you start to complain.

Stop yourself in midsentence if necessary. If you catch yourself complaining about a problem you can correct, take action.

If the situation is one you are powerless to change, ask God to help you see the good and to rejoice in Him.

Memorize Phil. 4:4 and repeat it often until your attitude becomes one of praise and rejoicing instead of murmuring and complaining.

## Scripture for This Week

(PHIL. 2:1-18)

Read this passage of Scripture daily this week.
Choose a few verses each day to pray.

## Praying Scripture

(PHIL. 2:14 AND 4:4)

*Holy Spirit,*

*Make me aware of my grumbling. Help me to stop, think, and pray. No one enjoys being around a complainer and grumbler. Philippians 4:4 says to rejoice in the Lord always. I want to replace complaining with rejoicing. Give me a rejoicing, praying spirit. Amen.*

### Song from Philippians 2:14

Do everything without complaining,
Arguing and quarreling too.
Eliminate grumbling, murmuring, and disputing
So that others may see God's work in you.
Do everything, everything,
Everything, everything,
Without complaining, complaining,
Complaining, complaining.
No arguing and quarreling,
No grumbling and murmuring;
So that others may see God's work in you.

# UNITE
# FOR RESULTS

I have just returned from a "prayer overnight" with a group of friends I met more than 20 years ago. We all attended the same church at one time, but our paths have gone in different directions. We no longer spend time with one another regularly. I haven't seen some of these ladies for five or six years. We laughed together, cried together, and came away invigorated by our extended time of prayer.

Although we met for the purpose of praying for ourselves and our families, we were enriched by the Christian fellowship and strengthened by praying together. This soul-baring, friendship-deepening event changed each of us.

In the past several years I have led more than 20 similar life-transforming prayer retreats for women in leadership, pastor's wives, college classmates, Christian friends, and others. Each retreat has been life-changing for me and for those who attended. There is power in praying together!

In Acts 16:6-15, the apostle Paul was led by the Holy Spirit to a small group of women gathered by the riverside for prayer. Through these praying women, revival spread through Europe. Praying together for a common purpose has incredible results.

There are many examples throughout history of prayer groups that committed to pray fervently for a stated cause and to persevere until the answer came. Praying Hyde and the Punjab Prayer Union prayed for spiritual awakening in Northern India, and after 12 years of difficult missionary service, an awakening came; 400 believers were added to the church. Amy Carmichael gathered seven women around her called Sisters of the Common Life to serve as spiritual partners in her missionary endeavor devoted to saving little girls from temple prostitution by establishing an orphanage. Stories of the life of Reese Howell reveal amazing miracles in Europe as a result of united intercessory prayer. Today, prayer groups are forming around the world to intercede for the nations that God's glory may be revealed in a mighty way.

At Pentecost, Christ's followers were in the Upper Room waiting in one accord when they were filled with the Holy Spirit—resulting in a changed world. You and I are called to change our world, and it can be done through united prayer efforts and obedience.

## Increase Your Spiritual Awareness

Ask God to help you choose a couple of prayer partners to meet regularly to pray. Each prayer partner can give the name of the person for whom he or she is praying. Plan to meet weekly or use three-way calling to pray for those three specific prayer requests. Agree to intercede for one another throughout the week in your private prayers.

Plan prayer walks with one or two partners to pray for yourselves and your families.

Consider organizing a prayer retreat for the purpose of extended, in-depth prayer.

Establish a confidentiality rule for all prayer sessions.

Pray your requests rather than talking about them. Maximize your time together. Seek direction from God as to how to pray for each individual and situation. Also, pray there will be no wasted or unhelpful words spoken.

Consider organizing a Lydia Prayer Group or an Apostle Paul Prayer Group. Choose whatever name you like, but commit to pray in unity with other believers. For information on Lydia Prayer Groups go to www.francisasburysociety.com and look under Titus Women.

If there are persons in your group who are too shy to pray aloud, encourage them to pray written prayers.

Stormie Omartian has a series of books on the power of prayer that includes published prayers at the end of each chapter: *The Power of the Praying Parent, The Power of the Praying Wife, The Power of the Praying Husband, The Power of the Praying Nation, The Power of Praying Together,* and others.

"Again, I tell you that if two of you on earth agree about anything you ask for, it will be done for you by my Father in heaven. For where two or three come together in my name, there am I with them" (Matt. 18:19-20).

## Scripture for This Week

(MATT. 26:36-46; MATT. 18:19-20; MATT. 7:7-8; MATT. 21:22; COL. 4:2; PHIL. 4:6-7; GAL. 6:2; 1 JOHN 5:14)

Choose one of these verses each day for your scripture focus. Read Matt. 26:36-46 each day.

## Praying Scripture

(MATT. 26:36-46 AND COL. 4:2)

*Jesus,*

*You were the perfect model of prayer. At Gethsemane, you gathered some of your chosen disciples to watch and pray with you in your night of agony, but they failed you. I do not want to be found sleeping when I should be praying. I realize that the results are multiplied when we join other believers in intercessory prayer. Prayer is work; it takes discipline. Show me how to make prayer a priority in my life; not just personal, private prayer, but unified group prayer. I commit to continue earnestly in prayer, being vigilant in it with thanksgiving. Amen.*

## Song from Matthew 18:19-20

If two of you on earth agree
Concerning anything you ask my Father,
My Father in Heaven will hear you when you ask.
He will do it for you.
For where two or three are gathered because they are mine,
I will surely be among them.
This is my promise, Jesus said to His disciples,
So gather and call upon my Father.

# CUDDLE
# THE BABIES

My husband was walking through church early Sunday morning believing he was alone when he heard a voice coming from the nursery saying, "You're so pretty; you're so beautiful. I love you. God loves you. You are special. You are so beautiful." He recognized the voice. It was Alpha, who supervised the nursery, and she thought she was alone. He peeked around the nursery door. Alpha was washing the dirty face and combing the tangled hair of a toddler who had arrived at Sunday School with her brothers and sisters on the church bus. My husband quickly realized those words may have been the only encouraging, endearing words that baby heard that week. Curtis has used that story many times to challenge children's workers.

Alpha Gibbs had come to my husband, her pastor, a few months earlier, asking to be involved in ministry within the church. When Curtis suggested the nursery position, she was elated. He knew she was qualified; she was a stalwart Christian grandmother who lived across the street from us and sometimes babysat our infant daughter and preschool son. Alpha filled that nursery with prayer and the love of Jesus. There were a number of newborn babies in the church, including mine, and more on the way. I remember thinking at the time that Alpha held the most significant position in the church.

I have often told church leaders and teachers in children's ministry seminars that the most important departments in the church are the nursery and preschool classes. Babies should sense the love of Jesus the first time they enter the church doors. Preschoolers are at their most rapid learning stage. Every opportunity to teach them of God's love is valuable.

Babies count. Uplift their parents in prayer. Are there babies in your sphere of influence for whom you can pray and extend love?

## Increase Your Spiritual Awareness

Pray over the nursery and Sunday School rooms used for teaching toddlers in your church.

Make a list of the people in your church who care for the babies. Pray for them daily.

Pray for the parents of infants and preschoolers in your family, church, workplace, and neighborhood. Their lives are often chaotic with heavy workloads that leave them emotionally and physically drained. Look for ways to help ease their loads. Ask God to reveal ways you can serve and extend His grace to these families.

When you read about a baby in the newspaper or hear a news report, breathe a prayer for that child and his or her family.

Pray in Jesus' name against the abuse of children. God's power can touch the evil hearts of men and women who crush the spirits of the little ones.

"If you are aware of a child who doesn't have a praying parent, you can step into the gap right now and answer that need. All it takes is a heart that says, 'God, show me how to pray in a way that will make a difference in this child's life.'"[1]

(MATT. 21:12-15; MATT. 18:1-9; PROV. 22:6; EPH. 6:4; COL. 3:21; DEUT. 11)

Read one of the above scriptures each day, and pray for children.

Read the entire chapter of Deut. 11, then return to verses 18-21 for your focus for the first day and the final day.

## Praying Scripture

(MATT. 18:1-6)

*Dear Loving Heavenly Father,*

*I come to you boldly on behalf of the children you created and designed. Give me a childlike faith and honesty. I want to welcome little children as you did. My prayer is that I will never cause one of these little ones to sin. Amen.*

## Song from Matthew 18:3-6

Unless you turn from your sins
And become as little children,
You will not enter the Kingdom,
The Kingdom of Heaven.
Anyone who is humble as a child
Is greatest in the Kingdom of Heaven.
Anyone who welcomes a child on my behalf
Is truly welcoming Me.

# INVITE SCRIPTURE TO SHAPE YOUR LIFE

It was a beautiful, sunny afternoon, so I decided to walk to a nearby shopping center to buy some greeting cards. I was mentally singing a simple song I had written from Matt. 19:13-15:

> Some children were brought to Jesus so he could lay his hands on them and pray for them. The disciples told them not to bother him. But Jesus said, "Let the children come to me. Don't stop them! For the Kingdom of Heaven belongs to such as these." And he put his hands on their heads and blessed them before he left (NLT).

Perhaps it was because the song was gripping my heart, or maybe it was because I was reading Gerrit Scott Dawson's book *Writing on the Heart.* Whatever the reason, I was strongly impacted by this passage of scripture. I began to visualize the scene and wondered what had been going on in the disciples' hearts:

Were they protecting Jesus after a hard day?

Did they think children didn't count?

Were they jealous for Jesus' time and attention?

Did they want Him all to themselves?

I imagined my grandchildren in the group being shooed away. I saw their crestfallen faces, their parents, my children, comforting them. But wait, Jesus is beckoning to them to come to Him. Not only is He calling to them to come, He is smiling as He moves toward them with His arms outstretched. I remembered Marissa's prayer and pictured her running into His arms. Kiersten would be beside her father, shyly holding back. I could see Jesus holding Makaila on His lap with His arm around my grandson, lifting His hand to tousle Calvin's strawberry blonde hair from time to time. Kevin and Michelle, Lanissa and Clay were standing in the background beaming. What a sight!

Then I recalled my children, Kevin and Lanissa, as babies. Curtis and I had taken them to the altar at our church to dedicate them to God. I now envisioned us taking them to Jesus and placing them in His arms for Him to bless them. As my thoughts continued, I was the child being brought to Jesus, and He was welcoming me with a tender smile and outstretched arms. I could feel His touch, see the twinkle in His eyes, hear His soothing voice; I was there in His arms being blessed, and He was praying for me.

In the wee hours of the night I continued to experience this brief Bible story, and it took on deep meaning for me.

The following day at church I was still gripped by the powerful effects of this scripture. It was a deeply emotional event.

Gerrit Scott Dawson says, "The scriptures are a source of abundant life whose springs are in God."[1]

In Deut. we find Moses telling the people of God's desire for them: "Oh, that their hearts would be inclined to fear me and keep all my commands always, so that it might go well with them and their children forever!" (Deut. 5:29).

Later Moses gave these instructions: "These commandments that I give you today are to be upon your hearts. Impress them on your children. Talk about them when you sit at home and when you walk along the road, when you lie down and when you get up. Tie them as symbols on your hands and bind them on your foreheads. Write them on the doorframes of your houses and on your gates" (Deut. 6:6-9).

"The people were to keep the words of the Lord running through their minds all the time. Moses asked them to be in constant conversation about them. In this way, they would keep God's words in their hearts. In the Bible, the heart is not only the center of emotion or the essential organ of the body, it is also the source of will and thought from which all our actions arise. Moses wanted the people to write God's commands into the very center of their beings."[2]

Allow God's Word and decrees to begin shaping your life. Impress them on your children. Talk about them, think about them, sing them, commit them to memory. Whatever creative ideas you conceive to help you remember God's commandments and allow them to come alive in your life, apply them.

## Increase Your Spiritual Awareness

Envision yourself bringing children to Jesus. Think about the children in your family, church, and neighborhood; your friends' and coworkers' children; children you see on the news or read about in the newspaper.

Meditate on this story from Matt. 19:13-15.

Choose a Bible story and identify with the people in it. Allow your senses to see, smell, taste, feel, and hear what takes place. Open your heart to receive a new and personal message from the age-old account. Pray it and allow its message to come alive for you.

## Increase Your Spiritual Awareness

### (MATT 19:13-15 AND DEUT. 5 AND 6)

Read Matt. 19:13-15 each day. Take in every detail.

Read Deut. 5 and 6 in one sitting. Then choose one scene from these chapters to explore in your mind and senses, allowing it to shape your daily life and become imbedded in your heart.

## Praying Scripture

### (I COR. 6:19-20)

*Dear Jesus,*

*Even little children were important to you. The scene of you blessing and praying for the children as you placed your hands upon each head touches me deeply. Somehow this story helps me to believe that you are never bothered when I come to you needing your attention and touch. Thank you! Amen.*

### Song from Matthew 19:14

Let the children come to me.
The Kingdom of heaven belongs to such as these.
Jesus placed His hands upon the children's heads,
And blessed them as He prayed.

166

# SCATTER
# PRAISE

At breakfast one Monday morning, young Lanissa was telling Kevin and me about what had taken place in her Sunday School class the day before. Some of the class members were speaking unkindly to one another, and the teacher proposed that each child say something nice to the other class members before leaving. Lanissa had barely finished her story before she and her older brother were speaking sharp words to one another. I suggested we try her Sunday School teacher's suggestion before they left for school with bad attitudes. I asked Lanissa to go first since she knew how the idea worked. With a surly voice, she said, "He's nice." Her tone was unacceptable, so I asked her to try again with a sweeter voice. Kevin was looking in the mirror combing his blonde hair. Lanissa shyly said, "Well, he *is* good looking." Then Kevin spoke to Lanissa saying, "I think you are a good student; you are creative and smart." After I gave each of them a word of praise, they gave me a compliment. I could hardly believe my ears! They spoke thoughtful words of praise about things I never knew they even noticed. As Lanissa skipped up the hill to school in one direction and Kevin walked away in the other, I could see that his head was held high. He always had good posture, but that day his shoulders were back, and he was walking with confidence. I imagined he was thinking, "She thinks I'm good looking." No doubt Lanissa was replaying in her mind, "He says I'm smart. I'm creative and a good student." I felt happy the entire day because of the kind words my children had spoken to me. Can you recall a time when someone spoke a word of blessing to you? It still feels good, doesn't it?

Likewise, verbal abuse and words of cursing are devastating. I heard someone say today, "You're a good kid, but there's no market for good kids." I'm not sure what that meant, but I think the speaker was trying to be cute or just make conversation. Every word we utter has a message. Usually those messages are not neutral; they are either positive or negative. Sometimes messages are conveyed through a nickname. One family I knew had an appalling pet name for their daughter. I don't even have the heart to tell you what it was, and I'm ashamed of myself for never having the courage to speak to the parents about its potential damage. I'm sure this nickname will affect her for her lifetime. Another friend of mine overheard her own father say about her, "Can't she do anything right?" She has never forgotten it.

Grace Ketterman has written a recovery guide for verbal abusers and their victims. The cover jacket says:

> Verbal abuse does not leave any visible bruises. Although you can't bandage the wounds or examine the scars, they are there nonetheless. Dr. Grace Ketterman helps you understand what verbal abuse sounds like and feels like. Her descriptions will open your eyes to the lethal power of malicious and careless words spoken at home, school, work, and even church. This book will help victims and abusers stop the vicious cycle, heal the wounds, and recover self-esteem.[1]

Ephesians 4:29 says: "Do not let any unwholesome talk come

out of your mouths, but only what is helpful for building others up according to their needs, that it may benefit those who listen."

*Unwholesome* means detrimental to physical, mental, and moral well-being or offensive to the senses.

*Wholesome* means promoting health or well-being of the mind or spirit.

Do your words benefit and bring a blessing to others? Are you speaking words that affirm and bring honor to others? Listen to yourself today. Listen to your tone of voice. Is it kind and gracious? Also, watch your body language. What is it saying?

Such comments as: "He's a good preacher, but . . ." or "She's a good cook, but . . ." negate the compliment. Stop with the words of praise. Smile. Extend graceful words to benefit the hearer.

Yes, the words we speak make a powerful impression. I suggest reading *Silver Boxes* by Florence Littauer and *The Blessing* by Gary Smalley and John Trent for insight on speaking powerful, life-changing words to others.

## Increase Your Spiritual Awareness

Ask God to search your heart and show you if you have spoken one word of gossip, hatefulness, or unkindness during the past two days. Even if you feel the person deserved it, go to the person to whom you spoke those words and apologize with no excuses. If you do this every time you speak an unwholesome word, you will find yourself speaking offensive words less and less.

At least once each day this week, ask God to show you someone who needs a word of praise. Jesus gave us an example of speaking words of praise. He said of Nathaniel: "Here comes an honest man" (John 1:47, NLT).

You may be a person who isn't particularly verbal, or your family may not have given praise easily. If so, this may be hard for you. You can start by writing thank-you notes to express compliments to others. You may try practicing by saying words of praise to yourself about yourself or someone you admire. Step out of your comfort zone. Be genuine and specific. Start with one person to bless with words of praise today. Ask God to show you who that person is. Scatter seeds of praise in the hearts of those you love.

Add God to your praise list. In fact, start with Him. Speak words of praise to Him for His faithfulness, sovereignty, righteousness, wisdom, holiness, glory, goodness, graciousness, guidance, justice, longsuffering, purity, omnipotence, omnipresence, omniscience, love, mercy, provision, protection, peace, counsel, power, greatness, hope.

## Scripture for This Week

(MATT. 12:35-37; EPH. 4:29; PROV. 18:21; PS. 34:1)

"A good person produces good words from a good heart, and an evil person produces evil words from an evil heart. And I tell you this, that you must give an account on judgment day of every idle word you speak. The words you say now reflect your fate then; either you will be justified by them or you will be condemned." (Matt. 12:35-37, NLT).

"The tongue has the power of life and death" (Prov. 18:21).

"I will bless the LORD at all times: his praise shall continually be in my mouth" (Ps. 34:1, KJV).

Memorize Eph. 4:26 in your favorite translation.

(ISA. 6:3 AND EPH. 4:29-30)

*Dear God,*

*I first want to give you praise! You are a holy God. Holy, holy, holy is the Lord God Almighty; the whole earth is full of your glory. I want the words that I speak to be holy words, filled with your grace and glory. Do not let any unwholesome talk come out of my mouth. Cleanse my heart and mind so that no unwholesome thoughts will fester there and come out in conversation. Please nudge me to hold my tongue when my mouth begins to speak harmful words. I know that you are grieved when I say hurtful things to one of your cherished children. I want the words I speak to be full of grace and to benefit the hearer. May my words bring honor and blessing. Amen.*

## Song from Matthew 12:35

A man's speech reveals his heart.
A good man's speech comes from treasures deep within him.
An evil-hearted man is known by his speech.
You will give an account on the Judgment Day
Of every idle word you speak.
Your words now reflect your fate then.
Your words justify you,
Or by them you shall be condemned.
A man's speech reveals his heart.
A good man's speech comes from treasures deep within.

# ACKNOWLEDGE HIS PROTECTION

My friend was driving with her husband and two teenage children on icy roads in Illinois. She had to stop suddenly, and the car spun out of control toward the car stalled up ahead. She said she started screaming: "God, help me! Help me! Help me!" When her car stopped inches from the other vehicle, she exclaimed: "He did! He did! He did!" I can relate to that story; can you?

My daughter, Lanissa, her church friend, and I spent a couple of nights in Tulsa, Oklahoma, during spring break. We enjoyed our relaxing minivacation and shopped, ice-skated, and met friends for lunch before leaving for Oklahoma City and home. The girls had an appointment with their youth pastor, and our plans were to go directly to the church. It was windy as we headed west; an ominous feeling was in the air. We hadn't traveled many miles before the sky ahead became hazy. It looked as if we were approaching a fire in the distance. We passed signs warning not to drive into smoke. I considered our alternatives. It seemed strange that there were almost no cars on the road, and I wondered if the exits in front of us and behind us had been closed. The car was filled with worried silence. I wondered if I should stop as we passed the final McDonald's rest area on the toll road. I knew there were no other exits for miles. But if we stopped, we wouldn't make the girls' appointment on time. Several miles later, I saw the smoke. My anxiety increased when I saw police and emergency vehicles parked at an overhead pass along the lonely toll road. Soon we smelled the smoke, and I could see a thick wall just past another "Do not drive into smoke" warning sign. As I pulled over to the side of the road, I saw flames leaping through the dry grass near my tires. I was terrified. I remember thinking, "I never expected to die this way." I began praying aloud as I checked my rearview mirror and turned the car across the two lanes of highway onto the blazing grassy median. A police car appeared from the wall of smoke driving down the median through the flaming grass. We passed just as I crossed to the other side of the roadway and headed back to the McDonald's rest area. There were people there who had been waiting with trailers and boats for hours hoping for the winds to die down. An emergency helicopter that had made rescue trips throughout the day was parked next to the building. Sections of the toll road were closed behind and ahead of us. We called home and learned that firefighters had battled flames and rescued people all day as the winds spread the fire across the dry plain. Several hours later, when it was safe, my husband and son found a back road and came to meet us and drive us home.

Every time I think of that day I thank God for His protection, and I often wonder how many times He has protected me when I wasn't even aware of the danger. Admittedly, I am guilty at times of taking God's protection and faithfulness for granted.

Once when Curtis and I were vacationing at a private rest haven for ministers in Hawaii, I was impressed to thank God for

His protection before I fell asleep. I awoke around 1 A.M. and felt impressed to again thank God for His protection. I asked Him to make me watchful and careful and grateful for His protection. I also prayed for protection for friends and family who came to mind. I fell back asleep and was sleeping soundly when I heard Curtis slip out of bed and leave the room around 3 A.M. He told me later that he was resting in the sitting area enjoying the ocean breeze coming through the screened windows when he was surprised to hear a vehicle coming onto the compound. As he peered through the open window, a large, barefoot man left his jeep with a flashlight and began shining it into the cars of the sleeping guests. When Curtis called to him, "What are you doing?" the stranger ran to his jeep and sped down the long, private drive back to the main street. Curtis came to the bedroom, awakened me, and told me what had happened. Once again I thanked God for His protection and thought of the many times he has protected me in ways known and unknown to me. I intend to continue to give thanks daily for God's protection and make that my focus for the next few days as I pray for myself and others.

## Increase Your Spiritual Awareness

Focus on God as your protector for a couple of days.

- First thing in the morning, give thanks for protection through the night.
- After traveling, pause and give thanks when you reach your destination.
- Thank God for His protection at the end of each day.

After several days, choose another attribute or gift of God for your prayerful attention. Example: His provision. All our resources are from Him. Even the things we create are possible because of the intelligence and strength He has provided.

Thank Him for:

- food and clothing
- health and healthcare
- guidance and wisdom
- shelter and transportation
- employment and benefits
- blessings and privileges

Thank Him for His faithfulness, goodness, guidance, wisdom, holiness, mercy, and love.

## Scripture for This Week

(PS. 91)

Read this Psalm daily. Choose a few verses to memorize.

When my brother, a U.S. Army chaplain, was deployed to Iraq, he memorized Ps. 91. He used the King James Version, and I memorized it in that version also. Several verses were familiar to me; others were more difficult to commit to memory. To help me, I set it to music. Try creating a tune for the verses you are memorizing.

## Praying Scripture

(PS. 91:1-2)

*Dear Heavenly Protector,*

*I find rest in the shadow of the Almighty and live in the shelter of the most High. You are my God, and I am trusting in you. That is enough! You are enough! Thank you for your protection. Amen.*

## Song from Psalm 91

He that dwells in the secret place of the most High
Shall abide under the shadow of the Almighty.
I will say of the Lord, He is my refuge, my fortress;
My God. In Him will I trust.
My God. In Him will I trust.

# TRUST HIM

Two days before our daughter's wedding, after helping her move from her tiny apartment to her house and working on wedding details, I fell into exhausted sleep. I was awakened a few hours later with the overwhelming sense of the presence of Christ, and I wanted to burst into song:

"He is here, hallelujah!

He is here, amen!

He is here, holy, holy,

I will bless His name again."*

My husband was asleep, so I began to whisper the song. Curtis awakened, and I told him I was trying to remember the words to the song, and as strange as it may seem, he sang it with me.

"He is here; listen closely,

Hear Him calling out your name.

He is here; you can touch Him.

You will never be the same."*

Then Curtis rolled over and went back to sleep. I was still wide awake and very aware of the Lord's presence. I told Him I

*Kirk Talley, "He Is Here," © Copyright 1990. Kirk Talley Music/BMI (admin. by ICG). All rights reserved. Used by permission.

knew He was there to deliver a message to me, and I was listening. I sensed Him saying to me, "Trust me! Trust me with your daughter and her new marriage."

I recalled her dedication. I relived a scene from her college years when I was alone in my living room praying for my dear, free-spirited, strong-willed daughter, fearing that she would make wrong choices, and I rededicated her to God, mentally carrying her to the cross and leaving her in His care.

After her college graduation, she decided to stay in another city to work and live alone. I once again found myself struggling with my concerns as I knelt beside her bed in my home. God gave me very pointed words:

> You are no longer her parent. You have laid the foundation; she is an adult now, older than you were when you married and started teaching school. She is now her own parent. You will always be her mother, but your task is no longer to parent her, only to love, accept, listen, and most definitely continue to pray for her.

So two days before her wedding, God was asking me to trust Him—not only with my daughter, but also with my son-in-law. Jesus continued to gently remind me to trust Him with my son and daughter-in-law, my husband, our future, my career, my continued journey. I believe He was saying, "Relinquish control. I am out front leading; follow me and leave your loved ones and your circumstances in my care."

Relinquishing control and trusting—those are tough assignments. But, oh, so freeing!

Why did Eve eat the forbidden fruit? To gain control!

What is lurking behind every sin? "I want my way! I want to be in control!"

There are many forms of control: rebellion, passive-aggressive behavior, bossiness, emotional manipulation, nagging, stubbornness, _____; you fill in the blank. Control brings bondage! Think about it. Trusting God releases and liberates.

Each day we make choices to be in control or allow God to direct our paths. Pray for an added measure of trust this week. Trust the One who created you and knows you better than you know yourself. He loves you unconditionally, and He is all-seeing and ever-present. Listen closely; hear Him calling your name and asking you to trust Him.

## Increase Your Spiritual Awareness

This is the week to relinquish control. Allow God to reveal to you those things that you hold in your grip and refuse to give to Him for fear He will mess things up. Admit it. Let it go.

It may help to do something tangible as a symbol of letting go such as releasing a helium balloon to the heavens.

## Scripture for This Week

(PROV. 3:5-6 AND PS. 37:4)

Memorize Prov. 3:5-6

"Trust in the LORD with all thine heart, and lean not unto thine own understanding. In all thy ways acknowledge him, and he shall direct thy paths" (KJV).

Prayerfully read Ps. 37:4.

Use the concordance of your Bible to locate scripture passages on trust.

## Praying Scripture

(PROV. 3:5-6)

*Dear Precious Jesus,*

*Just as you spoke to me so tenderly before Lanissa's wedding inviting me to trust you, I believe you are again speaking that message to me in my present situation. I have no words to express how your holy presence impacted me that night. Your surprise visit filled me with awe. I heard you whisper my name; I will never be the same. I want to trust you with all my heart, even when I don't understand. It is my desire to acknowledge you in every thing I do and to allow you to direct my paths. Thank you for that promise. Amen.*

## Song from Proverbs 3:5-6

Trust, trust in the Lord, with all your heart, trust the Lord;
Lean not unto your own understanding.
In all your ways acknowledge Him, and He will surely guide
your footsteps.
Trust the Lord, and He will lead your way.

# EXERCISE FAITH

A few months before graduating from seminary, my husband and I agreed we would not accept a call to any church unless we received a definite affirmation from God. After more than 20 offers were extended and none met that qualification, we began to wonder if we were idealistic in our belief that God would give such a definite answer. We were the last graduating couple to make a decision, and a classmate commented: "What are you waiting for? You've already been offered the highest salary of anyone in our graduating class!" Curtis meekly replied, "We're waiting for God to lead."

The following Sunday evening I met an older and wiser friend in the church foyer. She asked about our plans after graduation. When I shared our circumstances, she assured me that God's timing is never too late. The next day Curtis received a call inviting him to be the pastor of a small home mission church in New Jersey. Although we had never been in the state of New Jersey and didn't know one person who lived there, we both knew without a doubt we had received the affirmation we were waiting for.

We had faith that God would lead, and we also had faith that He would go with us every step of the journey, and He did. We loaded a U-Haul truck and set out for a church, a parsonage, and people we had never seen for the lowest salary we were offered. We worked with fervor, and God honored our efforts. We have amazing stories of what God did for us during our years there. We loved the young church that gave us the opportunity to learn many lessons in faith and following God's guidance.

More than 25 years later, I was teaching a class using Henry Blackaby's *Experiencing God* Bible study. We were studying the chapter on faith that is based on Heb. 11:6. "And without faith it is impossible to please God, because anyone who comes to him must believe that he exists and that he rewards those who earnestly seek him." We were asked in the workbook to describe a time in our lives that required faith in God and we responded in faith. We were verbally sharing in class what we had written. I told the group the story of our experience in New Jersey and our move to Houston. Both moves were to places I had never visited. We moved without seeing the parsonage or knowing one person. It was like traveling to an unknown world with all my earthly belongings. After I shared those two stories, I pushed back my chair and leaned forward and said, "I do not think I could do that again!" You guessed it! Within weeks we were asked to take an assignment in Northern Michigan, a place neither of us had ever been.

At first I went through what Henry Blackaby would call a "crisis of belief." I thought, "This cannot be!" It is cold and snows hundreds of inches a year in Northern Michigan; I'm a warm weather fan. We would be 13 hours from the nearest relative and much farther than that from our children in Oklahoma and Texas. There would be nothing but small towns in that part of the state; and although I was raised in tiny communities, I had lived in the city since college. Curtis would no longer be a pastor but would be serving in an administrative capacity. This just didn't seem to fit us. However, after taking the matter to God in prayer, we both felt confident this was His call. The assignment was accepted without either of us traveling to see the area or meet the people.

Neither of us had been that far north. Curtis and I had driven through the state of Michigan years before on the way to a conference in Canada, and I had flown into Grand Rapids and Kalamazoo for speaking engagements, but that was still several hours south of where we would be living. We knew very few people in the state of Michigan and no one in Northern Michigan. Curtis went first to establish an office and find a home. I was coordinating a statewide women's conference and teaching school and didn't go until spring break several weeks later. It was the middle of March, and we were already mowing our lawns at home. The day before I flew into Traverse City, Michigan, 10 inches of fresh snow fell. We traveled to a church in Alanson, Michigan, the next day. They had received 18 inches of snow that weekend. Within a few weeks we bought a home, moved, and settled into our new surroundings. We loved it! We lived there for five years, and almost every day I told God and Curtis, "I will grieve so much when we have to leave this place!" I loved the people. I loved my job. I became a nature-lover like never before. Who can describe the beauty of the Great Lakes, sand dunes, and the quaint villages with their gorgeous Victorian homes? God's world is too marvelous to capture in words.

God's ways astound me! I often told myself while living in Traverse City, Michigan, that I would have missed this wonderful experience if I had not obeyed God and walked by faith to this unknown world. Yet, I still have so much to learn in this faith walk. When I read faith stories in the Bible, I come away shaking my head! Noah, Abraham, Moses, Joshua, Daniel, Elijah, Hannah, Mary, Simeon, Anna, Paul—their stories bolster my faith. I plan to read the faith chapter, Heb. 11, every day this week. Will you join me?

Henry Blackaby says, "When you encounter God, it will bring a crisis of belief. That crisis will require faith. Without that faith you will not be able to please God."[1] That sends me to my knees!

## Increase Your Spiritual Awareness

Prayerfully answer these questions from *Experiencing God*:

- Describe a time in your life that required faith, but you did not respond because you lacked faith.
- Describe a time in your life that required faith in God and you responded in faith. This would be a time when you could see no way to accomplish the task unless God did it through you or in you.
- What do you know God wants you to do that you are not doing?
- Why do you think you are hesitating?
- Have you ever wanted to pray as the disciples prayed when they asked the Lord, "Increase our faith" (Luke 17:5)?
- Take a few moments to pray right now about your faith and what God wants to do through your life.[2]

## Scripture for This Week

(HEB. 11 AND LUKE 17:5-10)

Read Heb. 11 and memorize verse 6. Repeat that verse often. Make a list of your faith heroes.

Meditate on Jesus' response to His disciples when they asked Him how to get more faith (Luke 17:5-10).

## Praying Scripture

(LUKE 17:5-6 AND HEB. 11)

*Dear God,*

*I sometimes think my faith is miniscule—like a mustard seed. As small as it is, I pray that you will enlarge it. I am humbled by the God-sized tasks you have given me in the past. To work alongside you is an honor. Yet, when I read of prophets and men and women of faith in the Bible as well as missionaries and Christian martyrs in more recent times, I realize how small my faith really is. My heartfelt prayer to you is that I will walk into the future with confidence and hope, obeying even though I cannot see the outcome. It is by faith I believe in you. Amen.*

## Song from Hebrews 11

Faith is the confident assurance
That something we desire is going to happen.
It is the certainty that what we hope for is awaiting
Even though we cannot see it up ahead.
Men of God in days of old were famous for their faith.
By faith we believe in God.

# FORMULATE A MISSION STATEMENT

While driving to and from school, I listened to a Christian radio station. One day I heard the station promoting a new book. I was intrigued by the short description of the book that explained the author's purpose was to guide the reader in writing a personal mission statement. I was very familiar with mission statements. My husband helps churches write mission statements; my school had a mission statement; I had read mission statements on business brochures. But I never thought of formulating a *personal* mission statement. Surprisingly, within a few days, someone suggested to me that I write a personal mission statement after I shared my dilemma of whether to return to teaching the next school year. I asked this counselor if she was familiar with the book mentioned on the radio—*The Path* by Laurie Beth Jones. She was not. When I asked about the book at the bookstore, I was told the book was not yet available. Without a guide, I began to contemplate my mission. I decided there were three things integral to my mission:

- I have a strong desire to learn. I knew I always wanted to be learning, discovering, and growing mentally and experientially.

- I am a teacher. I felt sure that whatever I was doing, whether I continued in a public school or not, I would use my God-given gift of teaching.

- I want to be remembered for things that count. My desire was to extend hope.

These three thoughts represented my mission: Learning, teaching, extending hope.

By the time I formulated my own mission statement I had forgotten about the book, but in light of my prayers and thoughts about my mission, I made choices that totally turned my life around. I resigned my full-time public school teaching job. I organized an after-school homework center at my church; attended adult literacy training, taking a couple of friends with me; organized a statewide Christian women's conference; and was offered a half-day position at a private Christian school working with a specialized group of students. All of these fit my personal mission.

A few months later as we were driving to see our children for Christmas, I remembered *The Path* and wondered if it had become available. I mentioned it to my husband, so his first stop on vacation was the Christian bookstore where he asked about the book, found it, and bought it for my Christmas Eve birthday. Curtis is often so excited when he purchases a gift for someone that he can't wait for the special day to give it, and he handed me the book as soon as he saw me, saying, "Here's one of your birthday presents!" Before I finished the first page, I knew the book was beautiful inside and out. I could hardly wait to read it, and once I started I couldn't put it down. Before we returned home from the Christmas holidays, we both had written a personal mission statement. My mission statement read: *My mission is to encourage discovery and to enlighten hearts as I leave behind a legacy of hope to those God places in my life.*

Laurie Beth Jones says your mission statement should be one sentence that is easily understood and can be recalled and recited at a moment's notice. She suggests using action verbs that excite you, and she says that a good mission statement will be inspiring, exciting, clear, and engaging. It will be specific to you and your particular enthusiasms, gifts, and talents; large enough to encompass a lifetime of activities; and should cover both work and personal life.

I recently returned from a retreat center where I encouraged a group of 20 ladies to write their own personal mission statements. To help them get started, I gave them some questions to think about overnight:

- What have you done in your lifetime that you think no one else in this room has done?

- What is your purpose in life? Your passion? Your dream?

- If you knew you could not fail, what would you be doing for God?

I also asked the attendees—besides thinking about and answering the questions I posed—to pour out their hearts to God and make a list of at least 10 strengths He gave them. We were to meet the next morning after breakfast to continue working on personal mission statements.

We laughed, talked, shared, played games into the night, then went to our rooms to complete the assignment and pour out our hearts to God.

At our session the next morning, we shared some of our strengths and learned that a few of the women could not compile a list of 10 strengths. After our evening together, it was easy to help others complete their lists. One lady said, "I feel like I'm boasting." I assured her that her strengths were God-given gifts and she could think of it as boasting about God. Another very talented lady could only think of three strengths and immediately others in the group began shouting her strengths until she had more than she needed.

We then chose action verbs and reviewed the formula Laurie Beth Jones suggests as a guide. Before parting to do individual work, we read some sample mission statements from *The Path*:

- Jesus: [All His activities flowed from His mission.] "To give life, and give it more abundantly."

- A man who is a labor relations expert: "To uphold, discover, and support trust, honesty, and integrity in all relationships."

- A woman who works at a cancer care center: "To inhale every sunrise, and look under every rock for the joy life has to offer."

- Homemaker: "My mission is to create, nurture, and maintain an environment of growth, challenge, and unlimited potential for all those around me."

- CEO: "My mission is to foster innovation, enhance cooperation, and create prosperity for all whom I serve."[1]

Although it was not the goal for everyone to complete her mission statement—only to begin the process—some were able to satisfactorily write theirs. One lady who is battling multiple sclerosis wrote: "My mission is to encourage, motivate, support, and share Jesus with those in adversity."

You, too, have a mission to fulfill while here on earth. Your main purpose is to glorify God as you carry out your uniquely personal mission. Here are some powerful words from Laurie Beth Jones dispelling the myth that you are not important enough to have a mission: "Physicists and scientists agree that even an event as seemingly insignificant as a butterfly in Africa flapping its wings can affect the atmosphere in Alaska."[2]

Here is another powerful quote to contemplate: "Every word we speak, every action we take, has an effect on the totality of humanity. No one can escape that privilege—or that responsibility."[3]

## Increase Your Spiritual Awareness

Do you have a personal mission statement? If you don't, this may be the week to begin writing one. Using the questions and guidelines given here, you could prayerfully start the process. If you would like more detailed instruction, read *The Path*.

If you already have a personal mission statement, review it this week. Evaluate your present activities against your mission. Do they correlate? Make prayerful adjustments if needed.

Evaluate the jobs you accept and tasks you agree to against your personal mission statement. It will give you direction and a sense of purpose for your life.

## Scripture for This Week

(EPH. 1 AND 4:1-16)

Read Eph. 1:3-14 and make a list of reasons to praise and glorify God.

Read Eph. 1:15-23 and pray this prayer for spiritual wisdom and understanding.

Read Eph. 4:1-7 and ask God to reveal to you your special gifts.

Read Eph. 4:4-13 and ponder what God has equipped you to do.

Read Eph. 4:14-16 and ask for direction in ways you can help others grow so that the whole Body of Christ is healthy and full of love.

## Praying Scripture

(EPH. 4)

*Dear God,*

*I know you have given me special gifts and abilities to use for your glory and have called me to join you in your work. To live a life worthy of your calling, I need your help. I want to become more and more like you and use my gifts to encourage others to use their talents to glorify and praise you. Amen.*

## Song from Ephesians 4

May I lead a life worthy of your calling;
Make me gentle, humble, patient, kind, and true.
There is one Lord, one faith, one God and Father
Who is over all and living in me too.
We are all one body. We have one same sweet Spirit.
We have been called to a glorious hope above.
We each have a special gift to use to help each other
To build us up in truth and teach us how to love.

# SAY NO

My life was chaotic. I was the mother of an infant daughter and a preschool son. My husband was a pastor, and as the pastor's wife, I had unwisely acquired too many jobs in the church. I taught a junior girls' Sunday School class, coordinated children's church workers, was women's ministries director, led a ladies' Bible study, played the piano for a mixed vocal ensemble, sang in the choir, frequently updated six or more bulletin boards, did one-on-one Bible studies and mentoring for new Christians, and opened my home and entertained almost every weekend. I was way too busy. No wonder life was chaotic!

I remember the day I walked from my bedroom down the hall toward the living room with my face and hands lifted heavenward and cried, "Lord, you have got to help me!" He instantly replied, "I am going to teach you to say *no.*" His words could not have been clearer if He had spoken audibly. I resolved at that moment to eliminate jobs I had taken because I knew there was a need or felt pressure from others and to pray carefully for direction from God before saying *yes* to any assignment, no matter how insignificant it seemed.

Not too long thereafter we moved, and I was able to start with a clean slate. Before the boxes were unpacked, I received my first request. It was the Sunday School superintendent asking me to direct the children's Christmas program. His approach was: "I know

you have done lots of Christmas programs, and we don't have anyone to plan one this year. If you don't direct the program, we probably won't be able to have one this Christmas." I responded that I
had never directed a children's Christmas program because we had
always had capable people who volunteered to do it. I added that I
had just arrived, had more than 60 boxes still to unpack, had not
learned the names of all the people, but I would pray and ask God
if this was something He wanted me to do. I explained to him that
I had committed to pray before agreeing to any new assignment.
He seemed satisfied.

On Sunday morning I went to church sick because I didn't
want to miss a Sunday service at our new church. We had accepted
an invitation to a church member's home for lunch, and I knew the
lady had prepared a big meal. I didn't want to disappoint her by
calling to say I wouldn't be coming. Later that afternoon, while I
was taking a nap, friends from another city dropped by unexpectedly, stayed for church, and came back to our home to eat after-
ward. I went to bed that night feeling somewhat better but very
weary. Before I went to sleep, I began planning the Christmas program. When God interrupted my thoughts and asked me what I
was doing, I responded honestly. He reminded me that I had told
the superintendent I would pray about my decision. It became
clear to me that God's answer was *no*. I asked Him to show me if
He had someone else for the task, and He reminded me of a lady
who was rather new to the church who had been very active in her
church in another city. I called her the next day. She had directed
Christmas programs and agreed to meet with our Sunday School
teachers at their monthly meeting later that week to begin the
planning. As a result of this contact, she started teaching a Sunday
School class in our children's department. From this experience,

God taught me that when He tells me *no*, He has someone else to do the job if it is a task He wants accomplished.

I find that many people are as hassled, frustrated, and burned out by their chaotic schedules as I was. Praying for direction and evaluating my choices against my personal mission statement brings order and focus to my agenda as well as peace and fulfillment.

Sometimes God says *no*; at other times He says *yes*. Even when God says *yes* and nudges me out of my comfort zone there is order, focus, peace, and fulfillment because I know that He will go with me and give me strength.

## Increase Your Spiritual Awareness

If you are feeling stressed and hassled by the responsibilities in your life, prayerfully do an inventory to see if there is something that should be eliminated.

- What jobs are you doing that you have taken on yourself or allowed others to thrust upon you without seeking God's direction? Do they fit your personal mission statement? Are these tasks someone else could do?

- Whether they are home, community, or church positions, bow out of anything that you feel is not God ordained.

- Now list the jobs in which you are involved that you know without a doubt God has given you.

- Ask God if He has any new instructions to give you concerning these assignments.

- Ask Him if He has any new tasks in which He wants you to expend time and energy.

● Work smart—eliminate busy work from your life.

He will strengthen you for each assignment He places on your heart no matter how big and frightening it seems to you.

## Scripture for This Week

(ACTS 16:1-15; I CHRON. 28; EXOD. 3:1-17; EXOD. 4:10-17; PS. 119:33-38)

Acts 16: On Paul's second missionary journey, the Holy Spirit said *no* when he wanted to enter the province of Asia and again when he started to enter the province of Bithynia. Instead, Paul was instructed through a dream to go into Macedonia. From there we read how the gospel was taken to Europe.

In 1 Chron. 28, God said *no* to David when he wanted to build the temple; He said *yes* to Solomon and gave him the God-sized assignment of building the temple.

Exodus 3:1-17: God gave a dramatic *yes* to Moses and pushed him way out of his comfort zone but promised to go with him.

Exodus 4:10-17: When Moses protested that he was not a speaker, God placed Aaron in the picture.

Read these biblical stories, then take inventory of the jobs you are currently doing or considering. Accept God's *no*, and without protest obey His *yes*.

Pray Ps. 119:33-38.

## Praying Scripture

(PS. 119:33-38)

*Lord,*

*I want you to be Lord of my life! Tell me what to do, and I will do it. When you say* no, *I will obey. When you say* yes, *give me the strength and courage to move forward at your command. Give me understanding. Sometimes I struggle to hear clearly what you are saying. Turn me away from wanting any plan but yours. Revive my heart toward your way alone. Reassure me that your promises are mine to claim. I trust you; I am devoted to you! Amen.*

## Song from Psalm 119:33-38

Just tell me what to do, and I will do it, Lord.
As long as I live, I will wholeheartedly obey.
Give me understanding; I shall keep your law.
Make me walk along right paths; I know they bring delight.
Turn me away from wanting any plan but yours.
Revive my heart toward your way alone.
Reassure me that your promises are mine to claim,
For I trust you, I revere you, I'm devoted to your plan.

# FOLLOW
# HIS CALL

My husband and I were in Tulsa visiting our son, daughter-in-law, and three active granddaughters. Our second day there we waved good-bye to the school bus that carried two of our granddaughters to kindergarten and second grade. Their sister, two-year-old Makaila, was in our bedroom playing when her mother called from upstairs, "Makaila, come here." I overheard Makaila say to Grampa, "She called me. I have to go." She scampered upstairs to answer her mother's call. The cheerful expression and lilt in her voice told us that she was delighted to respond. Makaila's willingness touched me and reminded me of several stories in the New Testament.

Simon Peter and Andrew were fishing when Jesus said, "Come, follow me."

"As Jesus walked beside the Sea of Galilee, he saw Simon and his brother Andrew casting a net into the lake, for they were fishermen. 'Come, follow me,' Jesus said, 'and I will make you fishers of men.' At once they left their nets and followed him" (Mark 1:16-18).

When Jesus saw James and John preparing nets and called them to come with Him, perhaps they said to their father and the hired hands as they left the boat, "He called us. We have to go!"

"When he had gone a little farther, he saw James son of Zebedee and his brother John in a boat, preparing their nets. Without delay he called them, and they left their father Zebedee in the boat with the hired men and followed him" (Mark 1:19-20).

Later, I thought of modern-day examples in two books I read, *The Torn Veil* and *I Dared to Call Him Father*. In each of these true stories, the Muslim converts to Christianity responded, "He called me. I have to go."

My daughter's prayer partner and her husband resigned their high school teaching jobs, sold their home, and raised financial support to train to go as short-term missionaries to countries they can only enter for the stated purpose of teaching English. Their only explanation was: "He has called. We have to go."

As a teen, I heard Him call me to initiate action to get a new church of my denomination organized in my town. My family was comfortably attending an established church two towns away. The church was organized and is still serving God and meeting spiritual needs in that small community.

On another occasion, as I was driving home from a women's conference in another state, I heard Him call me to organize and promote a statewide Christian women's conference in the state where I lived. He honored my efforts, and nine states and approximately fifty denominations were represented in the large crowd of ladies who attended. He called and I responded, although I did so with fear and trembling. Many times He has called me to serve Him in faith-expanding ways.

As frightening as it may seem to you to follow His call when He is stretching you far beyond your comfort zone, there are surprising rewards along the way. No doubt God's heart is glad when we hear Him call and immediately obey Him with a willing spirit.

## Increase Your Spiritual Awareness

Prayerfully read the story of Zacchaeus in Luke 19:1-10.

- Is your desire to see Jesus so great that you will overcome obstacles of personal weakness, jobs, and time pressures to make a way to see Him?

- Envision Him spotting you in the crowd and calling you to come down to see Him. Would you respond as Zacchaeus did? "He called me. I have to go."

- Imagine what it would be like if He came to your house or workplace today. Would it change your thoughts and actions?

- Make a list of some of the dramatic changes Christ's coming has brought to your life. Give Him praise for these transformations.

- Ask God what He wants to say to you through this scripture.

- Read verse 10. Pray for those in your family and circle of influence who are lost. Remind yourself that Christ is seeking the lost. He is seeking to save your lost loved ones. You can pray with confidence, knowing it is God's will for the lost to yield their lives to Jesus. Pray with boldness. Don't give up!

## Scripture for This Week

(LUKE 19:1-10)

Read these verses daily in light of the spiritual awareness questions and suggestions above. Listen for God's call and respond immediately with a heart that says, "He has called me. I have to go."

Also read Luke 5:2-11, 27-32 and John 1:35-51.

## Praying Scripture

(LUKE 19:1-10)

*Dear Jesus,*

*When I hear you call, I want to immediately and willingly obey. I sense that Zacchaeus had a longing to see you; he exhibited this by his creative solution to overcome his short stature. The scripture says he came down from the tree at once and welcomed you gladly when you invited yourself to his home for a meal. My heart would have been pounding as you called my name. The dramatic transformation your presence made for Zacchaeus thrills me and challenges me to reach out to others with your life-changing message of hope. You have called me. I have to go!*

## Song from Psalm 95

O come, O come, let us sing to the Lord.
Shout with joy to the rock of our salvation.
Come before Him with thankful hearts.
Let us sing Him songs of praise.
For the Lord is the great God,
The King of all Kings.
In His hands are the depths of the earth;
The heights of the hills are His also.
The sea is His; He formed dry land.
O come, let us bow down and worship Him.
Let us kneel before the Lord our maker,
For He is our God.
Hear Him calling you today;
Hear Him calling you to come;
Hear Him calling you to come to Him.

# COPE WITH CHANGE

Life constantly changes. In my lifetime I have lived in 27 homes and 3 dorm rooms in 19 cities and 11 states. I have attended 15 schools including 8 universities, taught in 9 schools in 6 states. I know a little bit about change. I have been a student, secretary, wife, teacher, youth leader, mother, and have played numerous other roles in my lifetime. However, there are much heavier changes than these.

I have encountered changes that brought discouragement and sorrow such as extended illnesses and death. Some changes bring joy—others, sadness. At times I have been adaptable. At other times, adjustment was long and hard.

Major adjustments come with marriage, divorce, death of a loved one, arrival of a baby, a child leaving home, moving, a new job, loss of home or business, illness, accident, etc. The list is endless. Minor adaptations are needed for everyday interruptions and events.

The changes we choose may not be any easier than the ones we cannot control. There is no one-size-fits-all answer for coping with change. However, I have used a formula through the years that helps me when I face change. Some of the tools that work for me I have already talked about in this book.

### Read

Flood your mind with scripture. Ask God for a specific verse or passage for the change you are presently facing. "The whole Bible was given us by inspiration from God and is useful to teach us what is true and to make us realize what is wrong in our lives: It straightens us out and helps us do what is right. It is God's way of making us well prepared at every point" (2 Tim. 3:16, LB).

It is helpful to read God's Word and His promises as well as books He has inspired others to write. When we read stories of those who have conquered life's hurts and disappointments, it gives us courage.

### Write

I have encouraged you to journal. There is therapeutic value in writing about your experiences. Don't worry about spelling, punctuation, or grammar. These entries are for your eyes and benefit only. Use the means comfortable for you whether it is pen and paper or computer. Dialogue with yourself or with God. Answer the questions you have about a decision you have to make. List the pros and cons. Be very honest and keep your journal a private matter.

### Walk

Literal walking is healthy and an excellent tension reliever. Consider making it part of your daily routine even if it is only 20 minutes.

Another walk that we talked about in Week 15 is a prayer walk in your mind and heart through the past to the present. Dealing with the past gives us liberty to face the present.

## Talk

Talk to God in prayer. It is all right, even helpful, to talk aloud to God or yourself in the shower, journaling, or taking your prayer walk. There is something about getting the words out that has internal value.

Also, ask God to lead you to someone neutral such as your pastor, a counselor, a trusted Christian, or even a trustworthy support group. Finding someone you trust who listens to you and gives you prayer support is another aid in facing life's changes.

Speak words of praise to God. Sing uplifting songs. Say scripture aloud, and do not discount the value of laughter.

## Eat

So much of how we cope with change and disappointment depends on what we eat. In times of stress, we need even more good nutrients in our systems. Remember Daniel? If you aren't familiar with that story, read it for yourself in Dan. 1.

When we face difficult and stressful times, we often have no appetite, or we eat fast food and junk food on the run. Take time to sit down in a quiet place at regular times and eat balanced, healthy meals. Visit a nutritionist or dietitian if you need advice for a healthy eating plan. Your body is the temple of the Holy Spirit (1 Cor. 3:16). Treat it well.

## Sleep

We need rest most during times of stress and change. The psalmist suggests that God wants His children to get proper rest (Ps. 127:2). That is basic to coping with change. Even if you cannot sleep, go to bed on a regular schedule and spend the time before sleep comes praying and breathing in God's peace.

### Give

Find a place of ministry to others. When you are giving, you are also receiving.

- Write a letter of encouragement to someone.
- Make a phone call or visit a shut-in.
- Develop a prayer ministry for others.
- Start a Bible study in your home.
- Write a poem.
- Practice hospitality in your home.
- Give a smile, a listening ear, an encouraging word.
- Let God's Spirit flow through you.

Do not withdraw from life and become bitter, frightened, and emotionally shriveled. Use your change as a means of personal growth and benefit to others.

When Lanissa was two years old she fell and hurt her knee. She was crying, and I sat down on the floor beside her to comfort her. I held her, kissed her knee, brushed back her hair and spoke softly to her, but when I started to wipe the tears from her cheeks, she said, "Don't dry my tears; I'm not through crying yet!"

It is important to grieve our losses, allowing God and others to comfort us. When the time comes, we will dry our tears and face the day. We will be ready to give new hope to fellow strugglers.

## Increase Your Spiritual Awareness

Day 1: Choose a scripture for this week and try to read at least 10 pages in a helpful book.

Day 2: Write a page in your journal that starts, "My spiritual journey is like . . ." Write about some issues you are facing right now. Read a few of your past entries. Read Week 3 again, "Your Spiritual Walk Journal."

Day 3: Take a 30-minute prayer walk. Read Week 15 again, "Remove the Baggage."

Day 4: Talk to God aloud about decisions you face. Schedule an appointment to talk to another wise person.

Day 5: Choose to eat a well-balanced diet today. At each meal, make your prayer of blessing meaningful rather than routine.

Day 6: Commit to getting plenty of rest. Spend some time in prayer and some time reading before going to sleep. If you don't fall asleep right away, spend those minutes giving thanks to God and counting your blessings.

Day 7: Make this a day for giving something of yourself to someone else.

Choose to make your life a prayer.

## Scripture for This Week

(2 TIM. 3:16; 1 COR. 3:16; 1 COR. 6:19-20; PROV. 3:1-6; PS. 127:2; 4:8; PS. 89:14-18; PS. 71:24; DAN. 1)

| | |
|---|---|
| Day 1: | 2 Tim. 3:16 |
| Day 2: | Prov. 3:1-6 |
| Day 3: | Ps. 89:14-18 |
| Day 4: | Ps. 71:24 |
| Day 5: | Dan. 1 |
| Day 6: | Ps. 127:2 and 4:8 |
| Day 7: | 1 Cor. 3:16 and 6:19-10 |

## Praying Scripture

(1 COR. 6:19-20)

*Dear God,*

*My body is the temple of the blessed Holy Spirit. I want to make every room of my heart available to you. Show me how to care for this body and bring glory to you by the way I walk, talk, and live, no matter what changes I am facing. Amen.*

### Song from 1 Corinthians 6:19-20

My body is the temple of the blessed Holy Spirit.
He lives within me and makes my heart His home.
God has bought me with great price and owns each part of
    my being.
For this reason I give glory back to Him.

# PRAY WITHOUT CEASING

From time to time I devote a whole day to prayer. Throughout that day I try to pray without ceasing. Today was one of those "put everything aside for the purpose of prayer" days.

During breakfast I prayed a prayer of gratitude for my food and savored each bite as I gave thanks for God's provisions.

As I showered and dressed for the day, I asked God to illuminate every corner of my life and make it crystal clear and pure.

Watering my plants gave me an opportunity to thank God for His lovely creation. The brilliant yellow mums reminded me to thank Him for the many varieties of plants God has designed for our pleasure. My heart was joyful.

In addition to my listening time and prayerful study of God's Word, I took a prayer walk through my home and prayed for the people and circumstances I was reminded of by the pictures, gifts, and treasures in my home.

I spent some time with photo albums praying for friends and family. I used a church directory to pray for acquaintances and names of people I don't even know. I also chose a couple of names from the phone directory.

When I received phone calls, I prayed for the person who

called and continued to carry the caller in my heart throughout the day. I also prayed for those who sent me e-mail.

I knelt and prayed for friends who are struggling. I prayed for the recent prayer requests I have received. I walked, prayed for my neighbors, and praised God. I paced and prayed for the lost on my prayer list. I gave thanks for answers to prayers and for those being answered.

I must say that it's easier to talk and write about prayer than it is to pray. Distractions and wandering thoughts can thwart the best intentions if we're not careful. I reviewed Week 9 and applied my own advice.

As I read Luke 10:27, I prayed for myself and asked God to show me how to love Him with all my heart, mind, and soul. I'm not sure I totally know what that means. I meditated on that passage and asked for spiritual insight to its meaning.

I share these ideas with you to remind you that the ordinary events of life can become prayers. Could this be what it means to pray without ceasing?

## Increase Your Spiritual Awareness

Set aside a day or even half of a day this week to pray without ceasing.

Touch your world through prayer. Don't give up. Even if your heart feels cold and prayerless or your schedule is filled with good things, stop and pray. Learn to pause for prayer when someone gives you a request or you are prompted to pray. Work and pray. Walk and pray. Watch and pray. Sing and pray. Sit and pray. Stand and pray. Kneel and pray. Prayer is your lifeline to God.

(1 THESS. 5:17; LUKE 18:1; PS. 55:17; EPH. 6:18)

Use four index cards or sticky notes and write one of these verses on each and memorize it this week. Tape one to your vanity mirror. Stick another one to the dash of your car. Put the third one on your desk, kitchen sink, or other work place. Tuck the fourth one in your pocket:

"Pray without ceasing" (1 Thess. 5:17, KJV).

"Then Jesus told his disciples a parable to show them that they should always pray and not give up" (Luke 18:1).

"Evening, and morning, and at noon, will I pray, and cry aloud: and he shall hear my voice" (Ps. 55:17, KJV).

"And pray in the Spirit on all occasions with all kinds of prayers and requests" (Eph. 6:18).

(1 THESS. 5:17 AND EPH. 6:18)

*Dear Jesus,*

*I want to follow your example of praying. Teach me what it means to pray without ceasing, continually, all the time. I want to keep on praying on all occasions with all kinds of prayers and requests and not give up. Amen.*

## Song from Psalm 5:1-3

Give ear to my prayers, O Lord.
Consider my meditation.

Give heed to the voice of my cry for help,
My King and my God.
For to you I will pray;
My voice you shall hear in the morning, O Lord.
In the morning I lay my requests before you,
And I will look up and wait in expectation.

# SAY THANK YOU

Yesterday I was shopping for a birthday gift for my daughter-in-law. I was in a specialty store that I visit infrequently, but I was looking for just the right gift, and I found it. The sales clerk carefully gift-boxed my purchase, and as I was leaving she asked if I would like a drink—water or soda—to take with me. I realized that this was a thank-you gesture for shopping in her store.

There are many ways to say *thank you*: reciprocating kindnesses, smiles, notes, or simply saying *thank you.* We teach children to say *thank you* almost as soon as they learn to talk, but adults sometimes forget to say *thank you* to children or family members—or God. Sometimes we hold back because we are shy or feel we should say more but don't know what to say.

I was shy as a child. I often felt gratitude, but I was too embarrassed to say *thank you.* When I was about four years old I was spending Sunday afternoon with a young single adult in our congregation. Her name was Amelia, and I loved her dearly. At the time I dreamed of changing my name to Amelia when I grew up. Amelia's mother was an invalid and neither of her parents attended church. They owned a neighborhood store that was attached to their home. When Amelia took me into her mother's bedroom to introduce us, her mother asked Amelia to take me to the store to choose a candy bar. I thought this was the nicest thing anyone had ever done for me. I felt very special as I took my time making my choice. After I chose a candy bar, Amelia took me back to her mother's room to say *thank you*. I vividly remember Amelia's mother lying in bed waiting for me to say it, but the words wouldn't come. After a little coaxing, Amelia gave up, and we left the room. The rest of the day was ruined for me. I knew I had disappointed Amelia. I went to church that night and sat on my father's lap deeply troubled. My gratitude had turned to remorse. As an adult I realize that Amelia and her mother must have known I was too shy to speak up, and I have forgiven myself. As an adult God has helped me overcome much of my timidity and has given me the courage and determination to say *thank you*, often even to strangers.

Take every opportunity to express thanks. Push yourself out of your comfort zone if you have to. Lift another person's load by just saying *thank you*. Say it often; say it with feeling; say it now.

## Increase Your Spiritual Awareness

List 10 or more thank-yous to God.

Thank God continually today either aloud or in your thoughts. "Thank you, God, for the sunshine . . . for the ice cream cones . . . for a new day . . . for life . . ."

Concentrate tomorrow on thanking your family members.

Thank your son for making his bed, even if there are bumps and wrinkles. Thank your wife for the meal she prepares.

As the week continues, say *thank you* wherever you go, and turn your thank-yous into prayers of gratitude.

Sometime this week, send a note of thanks to someone.

(PHIL. 1:1-11 AND PS. 138)

How often did Paul and Timothy give thanks to God for the Philippian believers?

As you read this scripture, turn it into a prayer for someone dear to you. Make a list of the requests Paul prays for the saints in Philippi. Use this as a prayer guide this week for those you remember with thankfulness as well as for yourself.

Read Ps. 138 and express thanks to God.

(PHIL. 1:9-11)

*Dear Jesus,*

*It is a great joy to pray for the saints who have crossed my path. I pray that my love for them and their love for you will abound. Give us knowledge and discernment. Help us to see clearly the difference between right and wrong and to be clean on the inside. Fill us with the fruit of righteousness that comes through you that God may be glorified and praised. Thank you for your abundant blessings! Amen.*

## Song from Psalm 138

I give you thanks, O Lord, with all my heart.
I'll sing your praises and give you thanks.
Your promises are backed by the honor of your name.
When I pray you answer and give the strength I need.

The Lord will work out the plan for my life.
Your faithful love, O Lord, endures forever.
Your faithful love, O Lord, endures forever.

# WORSHIP THE KING

It was our first Sunday morning worship service in our new church. I sat on the second row near the center aisle and listened to the choir. The music was different than it had been in our previous church, and I was thinking, *I'm not sure I can adjust to this week after week!* I was pouring my heart out to God about it, and He spoke to me very pointedly. He said, "You did not come to worship the music—nor the preaching, nor the fellowship. You came to worship me and to join others in prayer and praise to me." God gave me His perspective, and it changed my attitude.

This week I have been asking God to teach me about worship. Today I read again a quote from Richard Foster that I have read many times before:

> When more than one or two come into public worship with a holy expectancy, it can change the atmosphere of a room. People who enter harried and distracted are drawn quickly into a sense of the silent Presence. Hearts and minds are lifted upward. The air becomes charged with expectancy.[1]

He then gives ideas of how to put this holy expectancy into practice:

> Here is a practical handle to put on this idea. Live

throughout the week as an heir of the kingdom, listening for His voice, obeying His word. Since you have heard His voice throughout the week, you know that you will hear His voice as you gather for public worship. Enter the service ten minutes early. Lift your heart in adoration to the King of glory. Contemplate His majesty, glory and tenderness as revealed in Jesus Christ. Picture the marvelous vision that Isaiah had of the Lord "high and lifted up' or the magnificent revelation that John had of Christ with eyes 'like a flame of fire' and a voice 'like the sound of many waters" (Isa. 6; Rev. 1). Invite the real Presence to be manifest; fill the room with Light.[2]

He continues:

Next, lift into the Light of Christ the pastor or persons with particular responsibilities. Imagine the Shekinah of God's radiance surrounding him or her. Inwardly release them to speak the truth boldly in the power of the Lord.

By now people are beginning to enter. Glance around until your eyes catch some individual who needs your intercessory work. Perhaps their shoulders are drooped, or they seem a bit sad. Lift them into the glorious, refreshing Light of His Presence. Imagine the burden tumbling from their shoulders as it did from Pilgrim's in Bunyan's allegory. Hold them as a special intention throughout the service. If only a few in any given congregation would do this, it would deepen the worship experience of all.[3]

I plan to follow Richard Foster's advice Sunday. When I bow my head to pray, I expect I will be kneeling, at least in my heart, before the King. I won't be criticizing the music or complaining about the temperature in the building or scorning anyone. I will be praising and worshipping! I will be asking God how I can present my body as a living sacrifice, a gift to Him. My thoughts will be lifted heavenward.

## Increase Your Spiritual Awareness

This week apply Richard Foster's suggestions on preparing for worship quoted above.

When you go to your place of worship this week:

- Kneel at the altar or beside a pew and present yourself as a gift to God.
- Stand at the pulpit and pray for your pastor.
- Go to the musical instruments and choir area and pray for those who play and sing. Pause and sing a hymn of praise to God.
- Sit at the pews and pray for all persons who will occupy those seats at the next service.
- Walk through the building praying for each Bible teacher and church leader.

Meditate on 2 Cor. 10:4-5 and 1 Cor. 2:16 and Eph. 4:23:

- Guard what you allow your eyes to see. Ask God to give you divine eyes to see others through His heart and eyes. Read Ps. 101:2-3.
- Refuse to listen to gossip, complaining, negative conversations. Excuse yourself if necessary. Read Phil. 2:14.
- Speak only words that benefit others, words that are full of grace and wisdom. Read Eph. 4:29 and Ps. 19:14
- Ask God to cleanse your heart and fill you with His righteousness. Read Ps. 51:10.

- Radiate His glory. Read 2 Cor. 3.
- Use your hands to bless and do good deeds in His name. Read Ps. 24:1-5, Ps. 90:17, and Eccles. 9:10a.
- Let your feet take you out into your world to live as His disciple. Read Eph. 6:15 and Isa. 52:7.

## Scripture for This Week

### (ISA. 6:1-8 AND MATT. 2:11)

In addition to the scripture used in the Spiritual Awareness section, read and pray daily Isa. 6:1-8.

Also read where the Magi bowed down to worship the Christ child in Matt. 2:11. Pause to worship Him.

## Praying Scripture

### (ISA. 6:1-6)

*Holy God,*

*I bow before you today saying, "Holy! Holy! Holy! You alone are worthy to receive my praise and worship." My heart sings! Teach me to worship you with my whole body and spirit. I wait in your presence. Amen.*

### Song from Isaiah 6:1-4

Holy, the Lord is holy;
He's God Almighty, and He is holy.
The whole world is filled with His glory.
He is holy.

Bow down before Him, for He is holy.
Holy is the Lord.
The Lord is high and lifted up,
His Holy presence fills this temple.
Holy is the Lord.
He is holy, Lord God Almighty.
Holy is the Lord.
Bow before Him for He is holy.
Holy is the Lord.

# CALL
# HIS NAME

It was Christmas Eve in Biloxi, Mississippi. My father was a civilian airplane mechanics instructor for Keesler Field Air Force Base. My grandmother had come from Tennessee for the birth of my parents' second child. Granny had a way of helping choose the names of her grandchildren and said, "If it's a girl, let's name her Patricia and call her Patsy."

Mother was in a Catholic hospital, and the nuns were singing "Silent Night" in the halls. Mother began to think it would be fitting to name the baby Carol if it was a girl.

I guess they both won, because I was named Carol Patricia. However, Granny went back to Tennessee and told all the aunts and uncles my name was Patsy, and I still go by that name today. But I've been called lots of names throughout my life. My older sister, husband, children, and students have all given me nicknames through the years, and I have accumulated quite an assortment of titles—a few I don't care to disclose.

I'm fascinated with names and how people acquire their names and nicknames. The meanings of names intrigue me also. A couple of years ago, I had a magnet hand-painted for each of my children and grandchildren with his or her name and its meaning.

Names carry significance. I put a lot of thought into the names for my children, but before I knew it, we had given them pet names. They are now adults, but we still call them some of those endearing names that originated from their childhoods.

Sometimes I reflect on the names God has given me: Beloved, His child, Redeemed One, Anointed for Service, Co-laborer, Daughter of the Morning Star. I also meditate on His names and choose different ones to call Him during my conversations with him. He is my Heavenly Father and Lord, He is The I Am, King of Glory, Eternal God. Sometimes I call Him Master, my Refuge, Creator of Heaven and Earth. Other times I call Him my Stronghold, Adonai, Jehovah, my Banner, my Rock, my Shield, my Provider. He is my Shepherd, Messiah, the Alpha and Omega, Ancient of Days, Anointed One, High Priest, and Bread of Life. He is the Way, Truth, Life, Living Word, True Vine, Dayspring, Counselor, Prince of Peace, Jesus Christ, Immanuel. This list doesn't begin to give all the names and descriptions of God, but it shows that there are many ways He can be addressed. Call Him by name because His name is Wonderful! And be sure to listen, because He is calling your name!

## Increase Your Spiritual Awareness

Choose a different name for God to use in your prayer time each day this week. Speak that name often. Meditate on it. Locate it in scripture. Whisper it. Say it softly. Shout it. Sing it. Lift His name on high.

## Scripture for This Week

Day 1: Gen. 17:1, Almighty God

Day 2: Isa. 9:6, Wonderful Counselor, Mighty God, Everlasting Father, Prince of Peace

Day 3: Luke 2:29, Sovereign Lord

Day 4: John 1:14, One and Only, The Word

Day 5: 1 Tim. 6:15, King of Kings, Lord of Lords

Day 6: Rev. 19:11, Faithful and True

Day 7: Matt. 1:21-24, Jesus, Immanuel

## Scripture for This Week

(JOHN 1:1-18)

*Dear Jesus, The One and Only, Divine Son of God,*

*You are my Sovereign Lord, my Shepherd, the Prince of Peace, Faithful and True. I bow before you in adoration. You are my Teacher, Counselor, Redeemer—my Stronghold, Hope, Refuge and Strength. I give you praise, my Lord and Savior! You are the Eternal Word who created everything there is. You are Life and Light. By believing in you and accepting you as my Savior, I am your child. The thought amazes me! You have revealed your glory, the glory of the only Son of the Father, full of unfailing love and faithfulness. Thank you for revealing yourself to me through all these names and more. Amen.*

## Song from John 1:1-5

Before anything else existed, there was Christ.
He has always been alive and is God himself.
He created everything that exists;
Nothing exists that He did not create.
Eternal life is in Him.
And this life gives light to all mankind.
His life is the light that shines through darkness.
And the darkness cannot put it out.
Eternal life is in Him.

# FEAR NOT

We were moving from Springfield, Illinois, to Houston, Texas. It was late January, and the mover had chiseled his van into our icy driveway and finished loading the truck after dark. A blizzard chased us out of the state, and the interstate closed behind us. We traveled to Kentucky and Tennessee to visit family before continuing our journey to Houston.

It was a Saturday evening when we arrived in Nashville and checked into a motel. Three-year-old Lanissa was not feeling well, and bath time revealed a severe rash. It turned out to be scarlet fever. I called a pediatrician I knew, and he met us at his office the following afternoon. After checking both Lanissa and Kevin, he concluded that they needed penicillin injections. We were driving two cars with two sick children and a dog. We made each of the children beds in the back seat of the cars, one driven by me, the other by my husband. Before we got to Memphis, my husband and I were both sick, and we had to stop again at a motel. The next morning I searched the yellow pages for a doctor who would agree to see us, and we ended up at a clinic waiting to be worked into the already-full schedule. Curtis and I took turns in the waiting room so the other sick parent could be in the car with the dog and the feverish, rash-covered children. After our double-dose shots of penicillin and extra penicillin tablets provided by the doctor, we drove a few more miles. Traveling a short distance and stopping to rest became our pattern for several days. By the end of the week, we were finally feeling better and planned to make it to Houston the following day.

It was our children's first time in Texas. I had been there once when I flew to Dallas. I had never been to Houston, didn't know anyone who lived there, had never seen the church we would be serving or the parsonage where we were to live. I told God I needed a verse to take with me into this new assignment. Although I had never done this before and can't remember doing it since, I picked up the Gideon Bible and opened it randomly and read until God gave me His promise. I opened to Isaiah. There are many wonderful passages in Isaiah, but I admit I don't understand all of it. I began reading a hard-to-comprehend section and decided to look elsewhere using my finger to save the original place. I had underlined many verses in my Bible while seeking God's guidance in making the decision to relocate and had the assurance that this was His will. However, the Bible I was now using was not marked; and after leafing through it, I decided to return to the page my finger marked. After a few difficult verses, I began scanning. Suddenly, a verse grabbed me. I couldn't have searched the concordance and found a more perfect verse for my situation. It was Isa. 41:10: "Fear not, for I *am* with you. Be not dismayed, for I *am* your God. I will strengthen you, yes, I will help you, I will uphold you with My righteous right hand" (NKJV).

I needed that verse the next day as I followed my husband into Houston in our little Datsun. A blinding rainstorm hit just as we arrived in the city. We moved from one vehicle-laden interstate to another until I lost Curtis in the traffic. I didn't know the way to the church where we were to meet members who were going to take us to our new home. Through my fears and tears, I claimed my verse.

Just before I reached the exit for the church, the rain subsided enough for me to spot the tail lights of Curtis's car. He was slowly approaching the exit ramp a couple of vehicles ahead of me. I still remember my great sigh of relief and the prayer of thanksgiving I whispered as we left the freeway and turned into the church parking lot where our new friends awaited our arrival.

The next day I was driving Kevin for his first day at his new school when he looked at me with a frightened expression and said, "I'm scared." I fully understood that feeling because I had changed schools almost every year during elementary school. Then I remembered my verse and told it to him. Even second-grade Kevin would understand those words. I explained that I had been afraid when I thought about coming to a new church and home and had asked God for a special verse. Then I quoted Isa. 41:10. I shared with him the thought that God would be with him to help him; and, as he walked the halls of the new school, he could imagine God being with him and holding his hand. This seemed to comfort Kevin; and when I picked him up from school, he reported a wonderful day. He never seemed to have a problem adapting to his new school, teachers, and classmates. I believe God answered my prayers and Kevin's by using that special promise from His Word; He calmed our anxieties with His "Fear not."

We find these words often in the Bible: "Do not be afraid." The angel said to Joseph in a dream not to fear to take Mary as his wife, and an angel told the shepherds to "Fear not" when the news of Christ's birth was delivered. Jesus told his disciples during the storm not to be afraid. On numerous other occasions, biblical characters have been admonished: "Fear not." Fear turned to joy for the shepherds. Fear turned to peace for the disciples. Fear turned to confidence for the psalmist in Ps. 27:1-3 and to hope in Ps. 23.

What fears do you need to lift to your Heavenly Father? Turn to His word this week and apply His promises to your situation.

## Increase Your Spiritual Awareness

Give God your fears as you name them. Talk to Him about them as you contemplate and apply His Word. Allow Him to calm your fears. Thank Him for times in the past when He has turned fear into joy, peace, and hope.

Explore some of the "Fear not" scriptures listed below and ask God to give you a promise for your situation.

Read the scriptures for this week as they are written.

Read them as if God is speaking directly to you.

In your own words, say the scriptures back to God in prayer.

## Scripture for This Week

Each day choose two or three passages from the following list to read and meditate upon:

Day 1: Gen. 26:23-25; Exod. 14:13, 20:20 Deut. 3:22
Day 2: Ps. 56:3, 27:1-3, 118:5-6
Day 3: Isa. 8:11-13, 41:10, 43:5-7, 35 (note v. 4)
Day 4: Matt. 8:23-27, 1:18-24 (note v. 20)
Day 5: Matt. 10:28-31, Luke 12:22-32 (note v. 32)
Day 6: Luke 2:8-10, John 14:27, Mark 5:21-43 (note v. 36)
Day 7: Heb. 13:5-6; 1 John 4:16-18

## Praying Scripture

(ISA. 41:10)

*Lord Jesus,*

*Reading the New Testament Gospels, I have discovered that you often spoke the words, "Do not be afraid." You did not want people to be afraid to come into your divine presence. In the Old Testament, I also find God often speaking to those who believed in the one and only true God, "Fear not!" I bring my fears to you today: fears about the future, my health, protection of my family —fears regarding challenging assignments you have given me— fears unnamed—nagging doubts. Although the words in Isa. 41:10 were spoken in another age to a different group of people, I believe the promise is also true for me as one of your followers. Thank you for your promise that you are my God and you will be with me strengthening and helping me. Amen.*

## Song from Luke 2:10; Matthew 8:23-27; Mark 4:35-41

"Don't be afraid," the angel said to the shepherds,

As the landscape shown brightly with the glory of the Lord.

"I bring you good news,

The most joyful news ever announced.

And it is for everyone.

The Savior, the Messiah, has been born tonight.

You will find Him in Bethlehem.

Glory to God in the highest heaven,

And peace on earth for all those who please Him."

"Don't be afraid," the Master said to His disciples,

As the storm raged around them on the Sea of Galilee.

Then He said, "Peace be still!"

And wind and waves obeyed His voice.

The disciples were filled with awe when everything was calm.

And said, "Who is this man?"

Glory to God in the highest heaven,

And peace on earth for all those who please Him.

"Don't be afraid," the Master says to His children,

As the storms rage around them on life's journey here on
    Earth.

"Be still and know that I am God.

I will never leave or forsake you."

Jesus, the Messiah, abides in your heart,

And He will give victory.

Glory to God in the highest heaven,

And peace on Earth for all those who please Him.

# PREPARE FOR HIS ARRIVAL

Yesterday during my listening time, God suggested I prepare my heart and mind for His arrival at a conference my husband and I are directing that begins today. All day I joyfully anticipated His coming. I prayed that those who attend will anticipate His arrival and sense His presence the moment they enter the grounds where the meetings will be held. I prayed for the speakers who will be sharing. My heart was joyful as I prayed, worked, planned, prepared, ran errands, and walked. I shared the message with several of my prayer partners.

I am bursting with excitement. He has assured me He will be coming to our gathering and asked me to prepare for Him. Not only will He be coming, He is already here in my heart. He will be there to meet me when I get there. He will travel with me, yet He is preparing for my coming. The thought amazes me.

All morning I have been thinking of Simeon and Anna and their brief story told in Luke 2. They had waited in anticipation for the coming of the Messiah. What joy they must have felt when they saw Him!

My thoughts turned to the message the Messiah gave His disciples following His resurrection and before His ascension. He told them to wait in Jerusalem for the arrival of the Holy Spirit. They obediently waited, and He arrived.

The Old Testament men and women of God awaited the arrival of the Messiah and the New Testament disciples waited for the coming of the Holy Spirit. Believers today await His return. I am compelled to believe that every day is a day to prepare for His arrival.

What might happen in our worship services if we prepared for His arrival? Would our day be transformed if we prepared for His arrival during our devotional times? Dinner would be different tonight if we prepared for His arrival at our table. Prepare for His arrival; rejoice in His coming. He not only came and is here, but He is coming again!

## Increase Your Spiritual Awareness

If you are following the calendar year as you read this book, it is now the Christmas season. Prepare your heart and home for receiving Him. Ask God what you can do to make this a holy week and what secular celebrations you can eliminate to de-clutter your days.

Invite Him to come to the activities of your life—your work, your play, your mealtimes, your celebrations, your quiet times with Him.

Prepare for His arrival.

Take Him with you into your world.

Scripture for This Week

(LUKE 2:1-40; LUKE 24:36-52; ACTS 1:1-11; MATT. 24:36-42)

Day 1: Read Luke 1:26-56 and Luke 2:1-20. Spend the day reflecting on Mary's anticipation of the birth of her son and her joy at the unexpected message she received as well as the surprising conditions of His arrival.

Day 2: Read Matt. 1:18-25 and Luke 2:1-7. Think today about Joseph and the extreme emotions he must have felt at the astounding news of the role he was to play in the arrival of the Messiah. Pray that you, too, will be obedient to God's direction in your life.

Day 3: Read the story of Simeon in Luke 2:25-35. Reflect on his excitement when he took Jesus in his arms after all the years of waiting and anticipating His arrival.

Day 4: Read the story of Anna in Luke 2:36-38. Follow her example of worshipping night and day today. Like Anna, find someone with whom to share the good news about Jesus. Ask God to reveal to you the name of someone who needs to hear from you about Christ today. Write, call, or visit that person as soon as it is appropriate.

Day 5: Read Luke 24:36-52. What is God saying to you in this passage? Have you, like the disciples, waited for the infilling of the Holy Spirit?

Day 6: Read Matt. 24:36-42 and Acts 1:1-11. Ask God what you need to do today to prepare for His second coming.

Day 7: Early in the morning prepare your heart for the Lord's Day. Worship and rejoice. He has come; He is coming again.

## Praying Scripture

(LUKE 2:36-38)

*Dear Jesus,*

*My heart has been touched as I have read the story of the prophetess Anna this week. Even though she was a widow and very old, I do not see her having self-pity. Her devotion to worship and prayer is a beautiful model to follow. I can visualize the joy she felt at seeing you after all those years anticipating the coming of the Messiah. She displayed that joy by telling others of your arrival. I, too, want to be a woman who prays, worships, fasts, and prepares daily for your coming. Thank you for coming to live in my heart. Show me how to spread the news that you have come to set up your kingdom in the hearts of men and women who will receive you. I anticipate your coming again. Amen.*

## Song from Matthew 24:36-42

Be prepared, for you don't know the day of my returning.
Only the Father knows the day and hour.
The Son of Man, He will come when least expected.
Be ready, ready at any time.
Heaven and earth will disappear,
But my words will remain forever!

# GIVE GIFTS

We returned from the glorious visitation of the Holy Spirit at our conference to a phone message telling us of the tragic accident involving our five-year-old nephew. He was hit by a truck going 54 mph and was lifeless when his father arrived on the scene and administered CPR. We reorganized our suitcases and hurried to Atlanta. Tyler was unconscious, badly battered, and remained that way for days. There was an amazing outpouring during those long days of waiting. Hundreds came to visit, some who had never met Tyler. A church donated a prayer pager that beeped every time someone called the number to indicate they were praying for Tyler; there were approximately 200 beeps each day, and that gave great encouragement to his parents. The hospital allowed the family to post updates from their computer and receive messages. Within a week more than one thousand messages were received from around the world. The small Georgia community where Tyler lived raised money for medical expenses through a benefit barbeque and concert. Donations were sent; one little boy baked cookies and sold them at his snack stand. People brought baskets of fruit, snacks, tooth brushes, word puzzles for Tyler's sisters, and more. People brought meals, printed maps and a list of hotels near the hospital, and ran errands for grieving family members who were preparing to travel to see Tyler. Teachers in the family were assisted by principals, other teachers, and assistants in preparing report cards, lesson plans, scheduling conferences, and other duties while they were away from their classrooms. The high school football coach brought Tyler a football signed by all the players. We were amazed by the creative ways the gift of mercy was extended.

And God was faithful to meet us at the hospital as He had met us at the conference. What a gift—the gift of His presence. He didn't have to give us a miracle, but He did. That, too, was a gift. I began to think of the many gifts He bestows daily—many that I take for granted. He is the greatest gift-giver. Even the gifts we receive from humankind come from a heart of goodness given by the Giver of Life. When we cannot see Him, He shows His face through the faces of people. He uses our hands, our lips, and our lives to join Him in His gift giving.

Let this be a week of gift giving.

## Increase Your Spiritual Awareness

Locate someone who is experiencing trauma and ask God to give you a creative way to extend a gift to that person or family. Pray daily and often for that troubled individual. Prayer is a gift.

If you don't know anyone in dire circumstances, go to the hospital, jail, nursing home, or cut an article from the newspaper. Pray for that person. If possible, find a way to connect. Give a gift of service. Ask God for a plan.

Notice someone who looks troubled, and ask them how you can pray for them. My friend, Monda, wears a prayer necklace with her two daughters' names in it reminding her to pray for them daily and for other significant people in her life. She travels extensively and on several occasions has found someone in an airport weeping and obviously grieving. Monda has taken these opportunities to gently approach the troubled person, explain her necklace, pray with the person, then give the necklace away with the reminder that she, too, can talk to God through prayer.

Give something away each day this week. Give lavishly. Give presents. Give hope. Give encouragement. Give service. Give time. Give yourself. Give love. Give treasures. Pray and give.

Read Matt. 2 prayerfully. Ask God to make you wise and discerning and ask Him to teach you how to worship Him. Kneel before Him now. Allow Him to search the deep corners of your heart and reveal truth to you. Pray a prayer of repentance if He reveals an area of disobedience, pride, or an attitude that is not Christlike. Give Him thanks for a cleansed heart. Ask God to align your faith with His Word. Offer Him the gift of yourself.

## Scripture for This Week

Matt. 2:1-12: The Magi brought gifts to Jesus.

Luke 4:16-21: Jesus quoted from Isa. 61:1-2 in the synagogue in Nazareth.

Isa. 61:1-3: Perhaps we, too, have been sent to bring good news to the suffering, to comfort the brokenhearted, and to announce freedom to captives.

John 10:10b: Jesus stated that His purpose is to give life in all its fullness. He is the gift and the greatest gift-giver. Follow His example.

Deut. 15:7-11: Give generously without a grudging heart.

(JOHN 10:10B AND ISA. 61:1-3)

*Giver of Life,*

*Thank you that you came to give abundant life. Thank you for bringing good news to me and for comforting my broken heart. Thank you for freedom from sin. Thank you for eternal life. Although I appreciate all your blessings and gifts, help me not to worship the gifts you give, but to worship you. Amen.*

## Song from Deuteronomy 15:7-11

Open your hand wide to your brother,
To the poor and needy in the land.
Do not harden your heart
Or shut your hand to your brother.
Give with cheerful heart and don't be grieved.
Because of this, the Lord will bless your labors.
In every work you do, the Lord will bless.
Do not harden your heart
Or shut your hand to your brother.
Give with cheerful heart and God will bless.

# INVEST IN YOUR DREAMS

Recently I had a vivid dream about an acquaintance I hadn't seen for 20 years. I hadn't even thought about her for many years. I seldom remember my dreams, but this one seemed so real I felt as if it had really happened and I had a real conversation with her. I began to wonder about her and prayed fervently for her and her family. I felt impressed to locate her.

Usually when I awaken from a dream about someone, I pray for that individual. I have no way of knowing the person's specific needs at that time, so I ask God to guide my prayers. If I have an e-mail address or phone number and feel led to do so, I try to contact the person.

Often as I am praying for someone during the night, I fall asleep. There was a period of my life when I felt that God was directing me to awaken and pray for the person I had been dreaming about. My husband is a light sleeper, and it's hard for him to go back to sleep once he's awake, so I told God that I would be obedient to get up and pray if He would take care of that problem. The next night I awoke from a dream about a person from my distant past. I quietly crawled out of bed and moved to the next room to pray. After about an hour, I felt released and returned to bed. For quite a period of time, the same sort of thing happened every night. Then one night as I was quietly getting back into bed, Curtis awakened and asked if I had been up praying. I knew God had answered my request for my husband to have uninterrupted sleep when Curtis told me this was the first time he was aware that I had been up. In the past he had been awakened by my slightest move.

I had an unusual dream one night in which I met a man I didn't know. In my dream he was distressed by the need to sell a piece of property. His name was the name of someone I had never met, but I had heard the name before. The next morning I asked Curtis if he knew this person. He not only knew him but was also able to tell me where the man lived and worked. I prayed for this man I had never met, and I asked God to reveal ways for me to pray for him. There were 18 specific points of prayer that I wrote in my journal in addition to any property sales or needs he may have been facing. I return to the list from time to time to pray for him.

I share these stories with you to say that I believe our dreams can be used as an avenue of prayer. I don't pretend to understand the complexities of dreams. Yet, when I remember a dream, I bring it to God to see if He has a message for me concerning it. I remember Joseph's question to the cupbearer and baker in Gen. 40:8: "Do not interpretations belong to God?"

In addition to biblical accounts throughout the Bible, there are numerous modern-day stories of ways God has used dreams for His purposes.

## Increase Your Spiritual Awareness

- When you awaken from a dream, pray for the persons in your dream if you remember their names.

- Ask God if He has any message to reveal to you through your dreams.
- Give distressing dreams to God and ask Him to remove them from your memory.
- Pray before going to sleep that God will guard your dreams.

## Scripture for This Week

(MATT. 1:18—2:14 AND JER. 33:3)

Read this scripture from Matthew paying close attention to Joseph's obedience.

"Then Joseph, being aroused from sleep, did as the angel of the Lord commanded him" (Matt. 1:24, NKJV).

"Now when they had departed, behold, an angel of the Lord appeared to Joseph in a dream, saying, 'Arise, take the young Child and His mother, flee to Egypt, and stay there until I bring you word; for Herod will seek the young Child to destroy Him.' When he arose, he took the young Child and His mother by night and departed for Egypt" (Matt. 2:13-14, NKJV).

Read Jer. 33:3. Although Jeremiah was not sleeping when this word from the Lord was spoken to him, he was shut up in the court of a prison. When we awaken from a dream, I believe we, too, can call on the Lord, and He will answer and show us great and mighty things which we would not otherwise know.

"Call to Me, and I will answer you, and show you great and mighty things, which you do not know" (Jer. 33:3, NKJV).

## Praying Scripture

(MATT. 1:18 AND GEN. 40:8)

*Holy Spirit,*

*I do not pretend to understand dreams, yet I believe there are times you have a message for me through my dreams. I give you permission to interpret my dreams for me, and when you do, I want to be like Joseph and immediately obey if there is some action you direct me to take. I will continue to pray for the individuals who appear in my dreams. If there is someone you want to lay on my heart, I am willing. Amen.*

## Song from Jeremiah 33:3

Call to me, and I will answer.
I will show you great and mighty things.
Call to me, and I will tell you
Secrets that you do not know.

# PURSUE YOUR VISION

What has happened to your dream? Maybe you've heard the joke about the man who went to the doctor and explained that he was having recurring dreams of a teepee and a wigwam and was worried about himself. The doctor replied with his diagnosis: "two tents." Yes, most of us are too tense; however, this is not the kind of dream I'm talking about this week, nor am I speaking of a nightmare or daydream. I'm referring to a God-implanted, inner desire of something you wish to achieve or a spiritual knowledge of something God wants to accomplish through you. What has happened to this dream or vision?

You may say:

- I've never had one.
- Circumstances destroyed it.
- Others shattered it.
- It was only a dream and, in time, faded.
- I'm working on it.
- My dreams have all been fulfilled.

What really happened to your dream? What is there deep down inside you just waiting to burst forth?

Paul said in Phil. 4:13: "For I can do everything with the help of Christ who gives me the strength I need" (NLT). That can be your assurance as well.

There are many reasons we hide away in a safe place:

- We're unwilling to step out of our comfort zones.
- We're afraid of failure.
- What will others think?
- The obstacles are too great to overcome.
- We are discouraged.
- We dwell on our weaknesses.

In 2 Cor. 12:9 we read this promise: "My grace is sufficient for you, for my strength is made perfect in weakness." Hannah Hurnard claimed that verse for her first speech when she attended Bible college. She had many fears and was afflicted with a severe stammer. When she learned she would have to give a speech to her classmates, her first impulse was to pack her bags and head home. God spoke to her and asked her to prove that His grace was sufficient for her. She obeyed with trembling heart. In her book, *The Hearing Heart,* she tells of walking to the platform:

I walked to the platform, stepped up on to it, and turned round and faced my audience. There they were, just as I had seen them in imagination in my little room at Keswick, a sea of faces, all looking uncomfortable and sorry for my misery. But as I stood, there, actually on the platform, preparing to obey the Lord, the thing that seemed a miracle actually happened. Every particle of fear fled. The moment I opened my mouth to obey the Lord, it was as though he almost visibly stood beside me, and was speaking for me. I opened my mouth and for the first time in my life I found myself speaking without a trace of stammer or even hesitation, talking just like everyone else. I said, "My text is, 'My grace is sufficient for thee, for my strength is made perfect in weakness.'"[1]

God planted within Hannah the desire to go to Bible school. He gave her the grace to break out of her shell; His grace was sufficient. He called her and gave her a vision of becoming a missionary, and His strength was made perfect in her weakness. If she had stayed in her shell of fear, comfort, and security, we would not have her books, her missionary service, her prayers, her sermons, her example. He can use you in spite of your weaknesses, handicaps, and fears.

What do you desire to do? Is it to make a speech, write, paint a picture, travel, run for office, complete a degree, or just take a class? Don't become too impatient. It takes time for dreams to flourish and develop. If there is a delay for some reason, use that delay to invest in the dreams of others. Joseph is a good example. He dreamed a dream as a young boy. It was many years, obstacles, and delays later that his dream was realized. But Joseph kept going, investing in the dreams of others, as God prepared him for what He wanted him to become.

It is never too late to set a goal or dream a dream. Grandma Moses was 76 years old when she started painting. Laura Ingalls Wilder wrote her first book when she was 65. Dream a dream even if it is a little one. Think of something you desire, then set a goal and write it down. Picture yourself accomplishing your goal. Tell yourself the truth: *I can do it. It may not be easy, but I can overcome obstacles.*

It is time for you, by His grace, to break out of your chrysalis and become the person you have the potential to become. His grace is sufficient for you. His strength is made perfect in your weakness!

One of the greatest gifts you can give yourself is to pursue your dreams and invest in the dreams of others.

## Increase Your Spiritual Awareness

Ask God to reveal to you His vision and purpose for you.

Prayerfully read this chapter again and allow God to expose any inner desire He has placed in you that you have ignored due to fear or personal weaknesses.

Ask Him to give you the faith and strength to accomplish your goal.

Memorize this verse: "Without faith it is impossible to please God" (Heb. 11:6). Realize that God-sized assignments require faith.

Take steps to obey His leading.

## Scripture for This Week

(PHIL. 4:13; 2 COR. 12:1-10; AND HEB. 11:6)

Memorize Phil. 4:13.

Read 2 Cor. 12:1-10 and reflect on weakness you may have that need to be given to God.

Read Heb. 11:6 and review Week 38.

## Praying Scripture

(2 COR. 12:9 AND HEB. 11:6)

*Dear God,*

*You have fulfilled your promise to take my weaknesses and give me your strength many times in my life as I have followed your call. Even so, I am sometimes afraid when you give me a new assignment. I want to have faith and please you for future God-sized tasks. Implant your vision within me. May it burn within me as by faith I walk forward to please you. Amen.*

## Song from Hebrews 11:6

Without faith it is impossible to please God,
For he who comes to God must believe that He is God.
He must believe God rewards those who diligently seek Him.
Without faith it is impossible to please God.

# REFLECT ON
# THE PAST YEAR

We have reached the final week of our year together. This is a good time to reflect and anticipate and to apply the Prayer of Examen to your life. This prayer allows God to walk with you to the depths, to search your heart, to examine your motives, to expose all. Richard Foster answers the question of how to practice the Prayer of Examen:

> With Examen more than any other form of prayer, we bore down deeper and deeper, the way a drill would bore down into the bowels of the earth. We are constantly turning inward—but inward in a very special way. I do not mean to turn inward by becoming ever more introspective, nor do I mean to turn inward in hopes of finding within ourselves some special inner strength or an inner savior who will deliver us. Vain search! No, it is not a journey *into* ourselves that we are undertaking but a journey *through* ourselves so that we can emerge from the deepest level of the self into God.[1]

Foster suggests there are three categories of prayer: Looking inward seeking transformation; moving upward toward intimacy with God; and focusing outward in ministry. If you have followed the suggestions in this book throughout the year, you have prayed prayers from each of these categories. We have prayed prayers of confession, repentance, relinquishment, request, and soul-searching for ourselves. We have lifted prayers of praise, thanksgiving, adoration, meditation, and silence to God. Our prayers have extended to others in forgiveness, intercession, petitions, and acts of grace. These prayers cannot be compartmentalized; they are intertwined, interlaced, and blended with the prayers of others as a part of a divine network.

After we have looked back and reflected, it is time to look forward with anticipation to the next year and the next avenues of prayer that await us.

I have been talking to God about a theme for the coming year; however, it hasn't been clearly shown yet. One year my theme was to develop a hearing heart. At the end of the year I felt I had made little progress, so I decided to keep the same theme for another year. At the end of that trying year, I felt I had developed a hearing heart and a new set of spiritual listening skills. Although these eternally valuable tools came out of dire circumstances, the lessons I learned from them were life-changing. Therefore, I encourage you to consider using this book again during the coming year.

My heartfelt prayer is that your life has been changed and that your relationship with your Savior will continue to deepen.

## Increase Your Spiritual Awareness

- Read again the first 10 entries in your journal and the last 10. If time permits, read the entire journal.

- Did you choose a theme for the past year? Review it. Prayerfully seek God's guidance for a new theme.
- Make a list of spiritual lessons you have learned on this prayer journey.
- Write a letter to God thanking Him for the lessons He has taught you this past year.
- Commit yourself to be used of God in the coming weeks.

## Scripture for This Week

### (PS. 139:1-18; PS. 139:3-24; AND MATT. 11:28-30)

Return this week to the scripture from Week 1, Ps. 139, giving careful attention to verses 23 and 24. Quote them often.

Review the scripture from the introduction:

"Are you tired? Worn out? Burned out on religion? Come to me. Get away with me, and you'll recover your life. I'll show you how to take a real rest. Walk with me and work with me—watch how I do it. Learn the unforced rhythms of grace. I won't lay anything heavy or ill-fitting on you. Keep company with me and you'll learn to live freely and lightly" (Matt. 11:28-30, TM).

## Praying Scripture

### (PS. 139:23-24 AND MATT. 11:28-30)

*Dear Heavenly Father,*

*I have given you permission to examine my heart and show me anything that displeases you. There is freedom in allowing you to search me and know my heart, you who created me and delicately formed me. You know when I am tired and weary and need rest. For this reason I can lift my burdens to you and know that you will help me carry them and lighten my load. Thank you for all you have taught me this year. You have called my name. I will never be the same! Amen.*

## Song from Matthew 11:28-30

Come to me, and I will give you rest.
All you who work so hard beneath a heavy yoke.
Wear my yoke;
It fits perfectly.
Let me teach you,
For I am gentle in heart,
And you shall find rest for your souls;
For my yoke is easy and my burden is light.
Come to me, and I will give you rest.
Come to me, and I will give you rest.

# END NOTES

## Week 4

1. Aletha Hinthorn, *How to Read the Bible So It Changes Your Life* (Kansas City, Missouri: Beacon Hill Press of Kansas City, 2004), 37.

2. Ibid., 6.

## Week 6

1. Dennis Kinlaw, *This Day with the Master* (Grand Rapids, Michigan: Zondervan, 2002), entry for August 1 (The Francis Asbury Society).

## Week 13

1. Byrd Baylor, *I'm in Charge of Celebrations* (New York: Charles Scribner's Sons, 1986), 1-2.

2. Ibid., 3.

3. Laurence Hull Stookey, *This Day—A Wesleyan Way of Prayer* (Nashville: Abingdon Press, 2004), 118.

## Week 14

1. Stormie Omartian, *Lord, I Want to Be Whole* (Nashville: Thomas Nelson Publisher, 2000), 54.

2. Ibid.

3. Ibid.

## Week 16

1. J. B. Chapman, "The Art of Forgetting," *Herald of Holiness*, April 22, 1936.

## Week 18

1. Richard Foster, *Prayer—Finding the Heart's True Home* (San Francisco: Harper Collins Publishers, 1992), 187-88.

2. Ibid.

3. Karen Burton Mains, *The Key to the Loving Heart* (Elgin, Illinois: David C. Cook Publishing Co., 1980), 148-49.

## Week 20

1. Irene Harrell, *Ordinary Days with an Extraordinary God* (Waco, Texas: Word Book Publishers, 1971), 40.

## Week 33

1. Stormie Omartian, *The Power of a Praying Parent* (Eugene, Oregon: Harvest House Publishers, 1995), 29.

## Week 34

1. Gerrit Scott Dawson, *Writing on the Heart* (Nashville: Upper Room Books, 1995), 11.

2. Ibid.

## Week 35

1. Grace Ketterman, *Verbal Abuse* (Ann Arbor, Michigan: Servant Publications, 1992), Cover Jacket.

## Week 38

1. Henry Blackaby and Claude King, *Experiencing God* (Nashville, Tennessee: Lifeway Publishers, 1990), 115.

2. Ibid.

## Week 39

1. Laurie Beth Jones, *The Path*, (New York: Hyperion, 1996), 63-69.

2. Ibid., 13.

3. Ibid., 14.

## Week 45

1. Richard Foster, *Celebration of Discipline* (San Francisco: Harper & Row Publishers, 1978), 142.

2. Ibid.

3. Ibid.

## Week 51

1. Hannah Hurnard, *The Hearing Heart* (Wheaton, Illinois: Tyndale House Publishers, Inc., 1987), 41-42.

## Week 52

1. Richard Foster, *Prayer—Finding the Heart's True Home*, 32.

# BIBLIOGRAPHY

Baylor, Byrd. *I'm in Charge of Celebrations.* New York: Charles Scribner's Sons, 1986.

Blackaby, Henry T. and Claude King. *Experiencing God.* Nashville, Tennessee: Lifeway Press, 1990.

Chapman, J. B. "The Art of Forgetting." *Herald of Holiness.* April 22, 1936.

Dawson, Gerrit Scott. *Writing on the Heart.* Nashville: Upper Room Books, 1995.

Foster, Richard. *Celebration of Discipline.* San Francisco: Harper & Row, Publishers, 1978.

———. *Prayer—Finding the Heart's True Home.* San Francisco: Harper Collins Publishers, 1992.

Harrell, Irene. *Ordinary Days with an Extraordinary God.* Waco, Texas: Word Book Publishers, 1971.

Hinthorn, Aletha. *How to Read the Bible So It Changes Your Life.* Kansas City, Missouri: Beacon Hill Press of Kansas City, 2004.

Hurnard, Hannah. *The Hearing Heart.* Wheaton, Illinois: Tyndale House Publishers, Inc., 1987.

Jones, Laurie Beth. *The Path.* New York: Hyperion, 1996.

Ketterman, Grace. *Verbal Abuse.* Ann Arbor, Michigan: Servant Publications, 1992.

Kinlaw, Dennis F. *This Day with the Master.* Grand Rapids, Michigan: Zondervon, 2002.

Mains, Karen Burton. *The Key to the Loving Heart.* Elgin, Illinois: David C. Cook Publishing Co., 1980.

Millhuff, Chuck. "The Brush." Used by permission.

Omartian, Stormie. *Lord, I Want to Be Whole.* Nashville, Tennessee: Thomas Nelson Publisher, 2000.

———. *The Power of a Praying Parent.* Eugene, Oregon: Harvest House Publishers, 1995.

———. *The Power of Praying Together.* Eugene, Oregon: Harvest House Publishers, 2003.

Stookey, Laurence Hull. *This Day—A Wesleyan Way of Prayer.* Nashville, Tennessee: Abingdon Press, 2004.

*Webster's New Collegiate Dictionary.* Springfield, Massachusetts: G & C Mirriam Company, 1980.

ALETHA HINTHORN

How to Read
the Bible
So It Changes Your Life

Let God's Word Change Your Life

Learn how to make *The Word*
come alive in the mundane,
everyday world we live in.

*How to Read the Bible So It Changes Your Life*
By Aletha Hinthorn

ISBN 978-0-8341-2137-9

BEACON HILL PRESS
OF KANSAS CITY

Look for it wherever Christian books are sold!

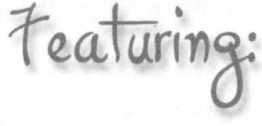
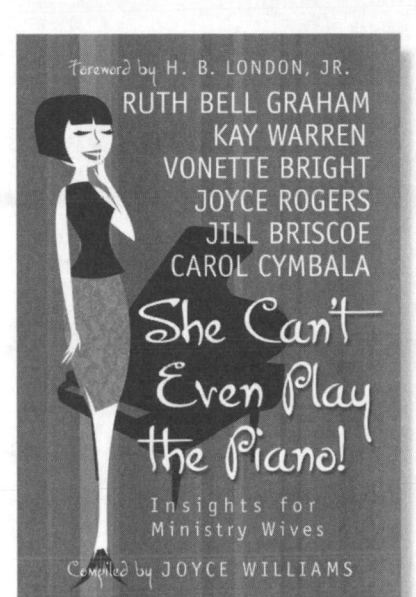

**Seasons of Prayer**
*Rediscovering Classic Prayers Through the Christian Calendar*
by Donna Fletcher Crow
ISBN 978-0-8341-1871-3

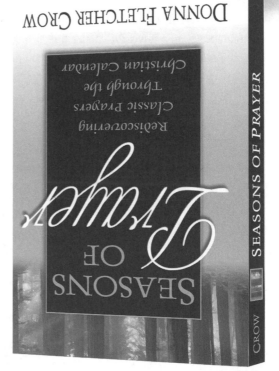

Grow spiritually and enrich your understanding of the culture and history of the Christian faith. *Seasons of Prayer* invites you to study the Scriptures and pray the classic prayers of Christendom through the seasons of Lent, Holy Week, Pentecost, Kingdomtide, and Advent.

# Inspired, Classical Prayers Woven into the Events of the Christian Calendar